glutton for pleasure

Menu

bruschetta
–
pan-seared
sea bass on
market succatash
–
stinky cheese

bob blumer

glutton for pleasure

signature recipes, epic stories,
and surreal etiquette

whitecap

Whitecap Books is known for its expertise in the
cookbook market, and has produced some of the
most innovative and familiar titles found in kitchens
across North America. Visit our Web site at www
.whitecap.ca.

Many of the recipes have been updated for this
compilation. Several from *The Surreal Gourmet*
and *The Surreal Gourmet Entertains* have been
rechristened. Some of the recipes and stories
previously appeared in some form in *Wine X
Magazine*, *Men's Health*, *Men's Journal*, *Maxim*,
Vice, *Highways*, the *National Post*, *Salon.com*,
*Adventures in Wine: True Stories of Vineyards and
Vintages Around the World*, on the CBC Television
show *The Hour*, and on the back of a Starbucks cup.

ILLUSTRATIONS AND OBJETS D'ART
BY Bob Blumer

All illustrations were hand rendered in acrylic paint
on Strathmore cold-pressed illustration board. The
original versions of the wine and martini glasses
were commissioned by the Salvador Dalí Museum
in St. Petersburg, Florida, for a fund-raising event.
They are made from standard-issue restaurant
glassware, cut with a ceramic tile "rod saw," then
glued to their base with five-minute epoxy. All
other pieces were fabricated from mixed media
and found objects. The guerrilla grilling mitt was
stitched by Susan Rose.

FOOD STYLING BY Bob Blumer

No food was harmed or manipulated for the
food photography. All meals were made by
the author exactly according to the recipes and
photographed (and subsequently devoured).
What you see is what you'll eat.

Photography credits are listed on page 263

Printed in Canada by Friesens

LIBRARY AND ARCHIVES CANADA
CATALOGUING IN PUBLICATION

Blumer, Bob

  Glutton for pleasure : signature recipes, epic
stories, and surreal etiquette / Bob Blumer.

Includes index.
ISBN 978-1-77050-015-0

  1. Cooking. 2. Entertaining. 3. Etiquette.
I. Title.

TX731.B5756 2010   642'.4   C2010-904310-3

The publisher acknowledges the financial support
of the Government of Canada through the Canada
Book Fund (CBF) and the Province of British
Columbia through the Book Publishing Tax Credit.

10 11 12 13 14   5 4 3 2 1

ENVIRONMENTAL BENEFITS STATEMENT

Whitecap Books Ltd saved the following resources
by printing the pages of this book on chlorine free
paper made with 10% post-consumer waste.

TREES	WATER	SOLID WASTE	GREENHOUSE GASES
45	20,814	1,264	4,322
FULLY GROWN	GALLONS	POUNDS	POUNDS

Calculations based on research by Environmental Defense and the Paper Task Force.
Manufactured at Friesens Corporation

For Mimi, whose legendary restaurant
inspired the aesthetic of my Toastermobile.
I can still taste your herbalicious hash
browns, "fluffed as a porn star" omelets,
and Blue Rodeo Chili. Breakfast
will never be the same without you.

contents

introduction

MY ACCIDENTAL CAREER began 25 years ago when my kid sister, Sarah, moved into her first apartment. As a housewarming gift, I cobbled together a small book containing a half dozen of my favorite recipes, a list of inexpensive pick-me-ups, and the best of my bachelor wisdom. The book was adorned with my own quirky illustrations and Polaroids of the dishes.

That was during my fledgling career in the music business. I was a glorified T-shirt hawker, touring North America with bands like AC/DC and Def Leppard. I was also managing the eclectic Canadian singer-songwriter Jane Siberry. The financial reality of being an aspiring music-industry mogul forced me to push my culinary resourcefulness to new limits. I leaned on the cooking basics I had taught myself in my college years, expanded my repertoire, and incorporated many of the survival tips I learned on the road. Between tours, I also learned that mastering a few dishes was the poor man's all-access pass to a girl's heart.

A few years later, as my music career evolved, I made the big move to Los Angeles—a city where everybody, down to the valet parkers, dreams big. During a lull in the action, while Jane was off recording an album with legendary producer Brian Eno, I embarked on a pet project that picked up where my present to my sister left off. My dream was to share my love of cooking and my secrets for living well beyond my means with my friends and kindred spirits. I still don't know if it was due to naïveté, tenacity, or good karma, but I managed to talk my way into the offices of Chronicle Books and walk out with a modest publishing deal.

In my ensuing quest to become the patron saint of dysfunctional kitchens, short attention spans, and mismatched place settings, I put my day job on hold, unplugged the phone, and locked myself up with a PowerBook and some art supplies. As the sparks flew, I committed my entire cooking repertoire to paper and accompanied the recipes with surreal food images I painted and pasted together in lieu of food photography—a luxury I could not afford. I also included a list of "music to cook by" for every recipe, which I believe was a first for the cookbook genre. Two months later I emerged, spent and exhausted, having channeled a fully formed cookbook. Well, it wasn't exactly a cookbook. It was a guide to better living that combined my passion for cooking with my knack for living large on a wing and a prayer.

Following the book's release, I was unceremoniously thrust onto the talk-show circuit. To compensate for my lack of culinary confidence, I incorporated an element of performance art into each of my appearances. (Don't know how to make a béchamel sauce? Learn to juggle lemons instead!) Much to my astonishment, the book was well received in the media, and was featured in the year-end roundup of the *New York Times Book Review*. The press coverage legitimized my new calling. I continued managing Jane for another six years until I decided to fly in the face of all conventional wisdom and quit my day job.

Since taking the leap, I've met and befriended some of the most respected chefs and winemakers on the planet. Through practice and osmosis, my cooking skills have caught up with my enthusiasm, and the mysteries of wine have begun to unmask themselves. Together these passions have spawned opportunities I could never have imagined.

And when my third book came out, instead of waiting for the phone to ring, I raised $250,000 from sponsors, created a Toastermobile out of thin air, and set off on a 17,000-

mile, 30-city, three-month odyssey to promote the book. The adventures from that tour and the Toastermobile itself became the genesis of my TV show *Surreal Gourmet*. Five years and 75 episodes later, I cut my hair, honored my love of adventure and übercompetitiveness, and rechristened myself a "Glutton for Punishment." That led to five seasons of food-related competitions around the world, a torn meniscus (with two resulting surgeries), seven Guinness World Records, and more than one near-death experience. I am currently at work on my third Food Network series.

The epicenter of all my recipe testing and dinner party "research" remains my Pee-wee's Playhouse–like kitchen, in which eccentric collectibles far outnumber functional appliances. This low-tech playground is anchored by a solid hundred-year-old butcher's block, a curvaceous refrigerator made by International Harvester, and an O'Keefe & Merritt gas stove with a loose door. Save for a few new toys and a lot of extra clutter, life hasn't changed much since I wrote that first book. Now I could probably acquire a set of stainless steel "trophy" appliances due to sponsors' generosity. But my kitchen stands as a symbolic reminder that making great food is all about ingredients, passion, and attitude—not restaurant-style, bazillion BTU stoves.

Many of the recipes in this book have been imagineered from scratch, and the rest were gleaned from a variety of sources, from street food vendors to three-Michelin-star chefs. Others are the results of my adventures as a Surreal Gourmet and a globe-trotting Glutton for Punishment. In order to make the cut, every recipe must embody my foodie philosophy: it's made from common ingredients brought to life with a liberal infusion of fresh herbs and spices, it requires little in the way of technology or expertise and is very forgiving, its fresh ingredients and creative presentation do most of the hard work, and it is instantly addictive, yet simple enough to be incorporated into any repertoire.

Those of you who are familiar with my work may recognize some changes in the recipes that follow. When I assembled this collection, I had to choose between being faithful to the originals and updating them. It turned out to be impossible to resist the temptation to explain a step more clearly or improve upon a recipe after having lived with it for several years—especially now that I *actually* know how to cook. I started by making subtle changes, then shamelessly moved into wholesale revisions, retesting, revamping, rechristening, and rewriting some of the recipes and content that follow. I also removed dated references, added some new favorite music to cook by, and reframed the recipes with some of my adventures.

The years since my first book have been the best of my life. I would not have had the privilege of living them the way I have if not for the encouragement of kindred spirits like you. Thanks for allowing me to venture off the eaten path by supporting my culinary endeavors.

For those about to cook, I salute you.

burnt toast

By the turn of the millennium, I had left my job in the music business behind, published two cookbooks, appeared as a guest on over 300 TV shows in several countries, and become a national spokesmodel for a major US food product. But in the world of promoting cookbooks, if you don't have a platform such as your own TV show or a high-profile restaurant, you are basically chopped liver. As I prepared to launch my third book, Off the Eaten Path, *with only a modicum of notoriety, I knew I had my work cut out for me. But I had no idea that the next little while would be the most physically, mentally, and emotionally challenging three months of my life.*

"No bread? Then bring me some toast!"
—*Punch* (British comic magazine), 1852

If you name a cookbook *Off the Eaten Path*, you'd better have a voracious appetite for adventure. At the same time, if you are a fledgling author trying to make it big, you should probably refrain from biting off more than you can chew. For me, the first of these conflicting principles won out, and that led to the creation of the Toastermobile—an Airstream trailer, topped with two 8-foot slices of toast, that served as my commando kitchen for the summer of 2000, and later as the set for my TV series *Surreal Gourmet.*

I had worked on my third cookbook for over a year, writing, developing recipes, creating one-of-a-kind culinary objets d'art, and toiling alongside the designer for two straight months of 14-hour days in an effort to create a uniquely styled book. By the end of the birthing process, I couldn't fathom the thought of handing my baby off to my publisher's jaded promotion department and embarking on the typical snore-worthy whistle-stop book tour. So I decided to take matters into my own hands. Why not go off the eaten path myself, I wondered, and inject a dose of high-adrenaline fun in the process?

In my former life, I was no stranger to the itinerant lifestyle, having crisscrossed North America multiple times in my various roles in the music business. Transforming a conventional book tour into a gonzo, rock 'n' roll adventure appealed to me—it was both practical and farfetched. I also secretly hoped that such a tour could catapult me out of the legions of niche cookbook authors into the big leagues, and maybe even lead to a television show of my own. These are, of course, the hopes, dreams, and aspirations of anybody who has ever published a cookbook.

In order to turn my dreams into reality, I channeled my love of travel, adventure, and cooking through my inner carnie. The result was a harebrained scheme to travel off the eaten path in some form of kitchen on wheels, one that captured the whimsy and lightheartedness of my new book but also emphasized my culinary passions by functioning as a serious professional arena. Instead of making do with the hot plate and crappy electric oven found on the sets of most TV morning shows, or simply yakking to food writers about my recipes, I wanted to invite the reporters inside my kitchen and involve them in some real cooking. And I envisioned my own pirate crew: a team of like-minded adventurers to help cook, clean, and drive.

One of my ideas was to customize an Airstream. I've always been a sucker for retro design, especially deco and atomic-age furnishings. An Airstream's aerodynamic profile and bright, aluminum-skinned exterior are a fusion of futuristic aesthetics and functionality. It encapsulates America's romance with the open road. Optimistic, adventurous, forward-looking: the Airstream and I seemed perfectly suited for each other.

If the folks at Oscar Mayer could transform a giant fiberglass hotdog on wheels into a national icon, why couldn't I come up with something equally unique? I mentioned my half-baked idea to Dick Kaiser, the simpatico photographer who helped me create the art for my first three books. Dick used to be in the ad agency business and has more creative ideas than Uncle Ben has grains of rice. He also likes to take the piss out of me, so I can never tell when he is serious.

After half an hour of amusing but fruitless brainstorming, Dick tossed another idea into the pot. "You know, those old Airstream trailers kinda look like vintage toasters. You could put two giant pieces of toast on top."

"That's it!" I cried as Dick laughed off the idea. To me, it was ingenious and I was instantly sold. As soon as I returned home, I printed a picture of an Airstream from a Web site and cut and pasted an image of two slices of nicely browned toast on top. Voilà! The Toastermobile was born—on paper, at least.

> ## "It was impossible, so it took a little longer to accomplish."
> —Wally Byam, founder of Airstream

A little research revealed that after a 20-year hiatus, classic Airstream models were once again being manufactured at the original Airstream assembly plant in Jackson Center, Ohio. Even the smallest Airstreams are fully functioning trailers with a bed, bathroom, kitchenette, and living/dining area. My quickly evolving game plan was to retrofit one so that the entire interior was a kitchen—and a highly functioning, self-sufficient, television-friendly piece of eye candy to boot. The model that most resembled a vintage toaster was the curvaceous, 17-foot Bambi.

I spend a lot of my time visualizing perfect-world scenarios, and then trying to make them a reality. From my naïve perspective, there was no question that Airstream Inc. would see my Toastermobile as embodying the spirit of Wally Byam, Airstream's quirky founder, from whose legacy I learned that Airstreams symbolized independence, freedom from routine, and a venturesome spirit. That is exactly what this tour will be about, I thought. In my mind, the synergies were obvious, and I was certain that once the nice people at Airstream heard my idea they would be only too happy to contribute a trailer in exchange for what (according to my delusions of grandeur) would amount to reams of valuable media exposure.

Unfortunately, the folks at the Airstream factory in Jackson Center, Ohio, saw my cross-country culinary crusade more prosaically. I didn't even get through the elevator pitch before I was politely informed that they'd heard—and seen—it all. Apparently people do the darnedest things with Airstreams. And while the polite gentleman on the other end of the line didn't want to discourage me, he certainly wasn't about to give me anything for free.*

To me, *no* is just a delayed *yes*, so instead of hanging up I asked to speak to their PR person.

"PR?" replied the man. "We don't have anyone like that here. I'm the corporate sales manager. If anyone has any requests, they come to me."

Mustering every iota of charm, business logic, and persuasion that I could, I kept talking, explaining the fantastic exposure the tour would bring Airstream. But the man on the phone remained unimpressed. When I hung up, I had to admit that in this instance, my perfect-world ideal would have to succumb a little to reality. I hate that.

I shook off this small defeat and pressed on. My fantasy promotional tour was snowballing into an extravaganza—a 17,000-mile, 30-city, three-month culinary odyssey, to be specific. The estimated price tag for the whole shebang had already climbed to $250,000. Yikes.

Seduced by the adventure, I was unfazed by the improbability of this plan and adopted a new mantra: go big, or stay home.

---

* To their credit, years later, Airstream Inc. did welcome me with open arms and support several of my endeavors.

One of my life secrets for making sure that I rise to meet a challenge that I've set for myself is to shamelessly blab about it to everybody I know. That way, my only option for saving face is to march forth with blind faith. By this point, I had shared my grandiose scheme with my publisher, my friends, my business manager, and my dad. So what's a house-poor, debt-ridden guy with lousy credit to do when he's in need of a cool quarter mil?

Punt!

I called a war room meeting with my friend-cum-business-manager, Norman Perry, and his business partner, Monica Netupsky. Together we came up with a list of every contact we had at any kind of company that might have been even vaguely interested in sponsoring the tour. During the six years since my first book was released, I had done promotional work for several food-related products, doing everything from convention demos to national television commercials. These products included some heavy hitters like Weber grills, Mrs. Dash spice blends, and Barton & Guestier wines. Our list started with the companies I was already in bed with and digressed from there all the way to Pampers.

Energized, the three of us spent the next week on the phone, using phrases like "unique opportunity" and "exclusive category rights." In addition to modifying recipes from my book to showcase their products, our pièce de résistance was my promise to wear a chef's jacket embroidered with each of their corporate logos—like a NASCAR driver's suit—for the entire tour. I loved it: a food tour that counted rock 'n' roll and Salvador Dalí as equal inspirations, with a bit of Hunter S. Thompson and Jeff Gordon thrown in for good measure.

After some understandable hesitancy, my publisher, Ballantine Books, agreed to kick in $20,000. It was basically their entire marketing, merchandising, advertising, and PR budget for the book all rolled into one lump sum. By giving me this money, they were essentially washing their hands of any further responsibility. That was a good start, but we still had a long way to go. I anticipated a lot of uphill work to raise the rest, but much to my surprise, almost everyone we approached jumped on board. In addition to much-needed cash, Chefwear agreed to supply clothing, Whole Foods our groceries, All-Clad our cookware, and Barton & Guestier the wine. Now that we had convinced the corporate world that this tour was going to happen, there was no turning back.

I called the sales manager at Airstream and ordered a Bambi.

Raising the money turned out to be surprisingly easy, but converting the trailer into the rolling kitchen of my dreams was, I quickly found out, "impossible."

A friend put me in touch with a small company in the San Fernando Valley that specializes in building custom kitchens for movie catering trucks and Mexican food wagons (which are affectionately known as "roach coaches"). The Armenco Cater Truck Manufacturing Company is run by a burly 63-year-old Armenian man by the name of Gerry Armenco. I called him and arranged a meeting.

Bubbling over with enthusiasm, I explained my vision for the Toastermobile. Gerry listened patiently until I was finished. Then, without missing a beat, he responded.

"It can't be done." His answer was curt and final.

"But what do you mean it can't be done, why not?" I stammered.

With the weary patience of someone who is explaining something for the tenth time, he continued. "See that?" Gerry said, pointing to a parking lot full of battered taco and ice-cream trucks lined up for repairs. "They're all square-bodied." He was right. None of them were anything like my voluptuously curved Bambi. "Everything that is made for catering trucks— sinks, refrigerators, stoves—is square. Your trailer is round. They do not make appliances or fixtures that would fit into it. They just *don't exist*." It sounded like Gerry emphasized the last two words to punctuate the end of our discussion. I thought he was going to turn around and leave.

"But—there must be a way to do it," I insisted, trying to keep the desperation out of my voice. I didn't know a damn thing about building kitchens or contracting or trailers or trucks, but I knew it had to be possible. It just had to.

"Even if it could . . ." He stopped.

"So, it *can* be done," I said, sensing an opening.

"Even if it could," Gerry continued reluctantly, "everything would have to be fabricated from scratch, by hand: the sinks, the floor, the counters, the water tank, the refrigeration unit. All from scratch. And all to code, to satisfy food safety regulations."

That was all I needed. Fifteen minutes later, Gerry and I had negotiated the price: $45,000. That was well over my nascent budget, but I didn't quibble. The impossible had just become the achievable.

In short order, the shell of my Bambi was on a flatbed rolling through the Rockies, headed for California.

I soon learned that Gerry had a heart of gold and the passion of an artist. It was my good fortune that he embraced the project as though underbudgeted, one-off designs in impossibly round vehicles were his true calling. From a few chicken scratchings on a napkin, he designed and fabricated a stainless steel kitchen with a Wolf stove, a custom-built refrigeration system, diamond-pattern flooring, diner-style quilted aluminum walls, and a pass-through window that was blown out of the starboard side. And per my Weber contract, Gerry jerry-rigged one of their top-of-the-line propane grills so that it could be locked down into the interior and off-loaded at every stop.

When it came time to fabricate the 8-foot slices of toast, Gerry was almost insulted that I didn't consider him first for the job. "You want to make those, too?" I asked, surprised that he had any patience left for my project. Suffice to say, he crafted two fabulous three-dimensional 8-foot aluminum slices of toast that would make Claes Oldenburg green with envy.

Shortly after my Toastermobile was finished, I had a big party, hugged my friends, kissed my flummoxed girlfriend good-bye, and climbed into a rented 40-foot Winnebago that would function as a rolling home and tow vehicle. Along with a driver, a sous chef, and an assistant/tour manager/photographer, I set off on what can only be described as an epic journey.

> "Some days you tame the tiger. And some days the tiger has you for lunch."
> —Tug McGraw

St. Petersburg, Florida, June 26. It's 5:15 a.m. and we are on day 22 of the tour. We have already traveled 4,300 miles, ticked off eight cities, and had exactly one and a half days off. Our days begin at dawn and end in bone-crushing fatigue long after the last dinner guest goes home. Crisscrossing the continent initially sounded idyllic, but visions of meandering trips down quaint backcountry roads and exploratory quests for the perfect barbecue joint have faded to only one desire: sleep.

Any free hours I am able to snatch are spent on my cell phone, doing interviews, pinning down schedules, juggling sponsor requests, finalizing details of media appearances, arranging drop shipments of supplies—all in my quest to save America from the evils of mediocre food, one palate at a time.

I'll sleep when I'm dead—that is, if this tour doesn't kill me first. It's not like I don't have help. There are a total of 10 other people who have become intimately involved in the organization of this culinary odyssey. In addition to the three-person road crew, the pit team includes Norman and Monica in New York, who are handling the financing and sponsor relationships; four publicists, who've divvied up the United States and Canada between them and are pitching like hell; and a home-base tour coordinator in Los Angeles. I am flabbergasted that the organization required to publicize a single cookbook could escalate, almost overnight, into a full-blown company. To top it off, PR people representing the interests of various sponsors parachute in along the way and add to the mayhem.

I do, on average, five events a day; mostly a mix of interviews, book signings, cocktail parties, dinner parties, TV appearances, and the occasional spontaneous drive-by shrimp tasting.

This morning we are up before daybreak in St. Petersburg. Our day is starting with a live television appearance on WTOG. Looming in the distance, we see a cluster of large satellite dishes on the roof of an industrial-looking building—the signpost of TV studios everywhere. We pull into the parking lot. Suzi Varin, the onboard tour manager/photographer (yes, the same person who shot almost everything in this book), springs into action and goes to find someone to let us into the studio.

From behind a smoky glass window, a security guard does a double take as his eyes focus on the Toastermobile.

So far the Toastermobile has functioned as imagined. Motorists honk approvingly, chefs covet it, and, most importantly, the media eats it up. Once producers see it with their own two eyes, they want to milk it for all it's worth—not just because it makes for a change from the usual in-studio cooking segment, but because it's fun. It makes people—even cynical, seen-it-all television producers—smile.

Suzi emerges with a chipper segment producer named Laurie, who informs us that I am

scheduled to go live at 7:12. Laurie walks me to the studio through a set of huge swinging doors, over which is a red light with a sign next to it saying ON AIR. A squat, surly guy with coffee and tobacco breath introduces himself as the sound tech and puts his hands up my shirt, running a wire down the front of my logo-covered chef's jacket.

Two stagehands roll cameras outside and illuminate the interior of the Toastermobile with a "sun gun" they rig to a small hook on the ceiling that Gerry attached specifically for this purpose. In a matter of seconds, everything is illuminated.

A minute before my segment, Laurie runs out and delivers the news that my allotted four and a half minutes of airtime has just been reduced to three. In an instant, I have to figure out how to explain why I call myself the Surreal Gourmet, start my Shrimp on the Barbie with Cilantro Dipping Sauce (see page 202), explain the origins of the Toastermobile, pitch my book, and have the shrimp done and ready to taste in less time than it takes to warm up a pan in real life. It's a bitch and a letdown, but there is nothing I can do about it. A tractor-trailer overturns somewhere, a hurricane watch goes into effect, or maybe the last guest just went over on their allotted time—and it's chop chop.

Jacki, the host, climbs into the Toastermobile, looks at me, and asks, "So what's your specialty?", making it evident that she has never even cracked the copy of my book she is holding in her hand. I am deflated. I look up to see the floor producer counting down. "Four, three . . . ," he says. Then he holds up two fingers, and points at me on the count of one.

The red light over the camera goes on, and on cue Jacki lights up. We banter while I demo the recipe. I do my best to engage her in the cooking process and get in all my key talking points. I'm just hitting my stride, when from the corner of my eye I see the floor producer roll his left hand in a circular movement indicating that Jacki has to wrap up the segment. She stabs the shrimp into the dish of cilantro sauce, which sits flirtily between a Barbie's splayed legs, and takes a dainty little nibble. Before even swallowing, she coos, "Delicious."

Jacki throws back to the in-studio news anchor, the camera light goes off, and we both relax. After a few seconds of small talk, she picks up another shrimp, dips it, chews slowly, then volunteers, "This really is delicious. I think it is the best shrimp I've ever tasted." For the first time, she is being sincere. And it kills me that no one watching the news that morning will ever hear her genuine endorsement or see the look of food-induced pleasure on her face. After she leaves, the TV crew swoop in like vultures to devour the leftovers.

With the segment wrapped, Mary Burnham, my sous chef, heads into the Toastermobile to clean up the shrimp tails and latch down the drawers. Mary—nicknamed Mary Sous for the duration—is a friend and fellow food fanatic from New York who came to my rescue after the

first sous chef (nicknamed Angry Man) was voted off the Toastermobile after just one week, in a real-life game of *Survivor.*

Come to think of it, the tour is making *Survivor* look like a Club Med vacation. Back in the RV, Phil, our Texan-based driver, dozes against a windowpane and Suzi multitasks while talking on her cell.

"OK, what's next?" I ask her as soon as she hangs up.

"We have a huge supply run to do at Whole Foods, followed by a tasting in their parking lot at 10:30, a book signing at a local bookstore at lunchtime, and a big dinner party for Barton & Guestier and their VIP guests tonight at 6." B&G is our wine sponsor, and I realize with a sinking feeling that nothing for the dinner party has been prepped, meaning it all needs to get done, from scratch, between the afternoon bookstore appearance and dinner—or *showtime,* as I call it.

"Let's go!" Suzi tells Phil and we head out through the burbs to a new subdivision of St. Petersburg, where we find the shopping mall. It's only 8:40 in the morning. The lot is empty and the store is deserted. Suzi looks at the clipboard on her lap, then at her watch. She looks up with a big grin. "Time for breakfast," she says gleefully. "But only if we can do it in less than 20 minutes."

Yeehaw! The combination of sleep deprivation and the post–adrenaline rush from the live television segment has made me ravenous.

"Hey kids, who wants Parking Lot Eggs?" I ask rhetorically. Mary takes the cue and we jump out of the RV and pile into the Toastermobile. Parking Lot Eggs is the name we have christened the mash-up of eggs and leftovers that I love to make for the crew on the rare occasion that we have time to eat breakfast. Mary starts rooting through the refrigerator while I pull a frying pan from my arsenal of All-Clad-sponsored cookware and ignite 5,000 BTUs of firepower.

Ten minutes later, we're sitting in a row on a concrete parking lot divider, digging into plates of scrambled eggs, pancetta, Parmigiano Reggiano, shallots, garlic, avocado, cilantro, and a pinch of my favorite ingredient of the moment, chipotle powder (see recipe for Parking Lot Eggs page 174). No fuss, no muss—all flavor. Five minutes after that, the emptied plates are scraped and in the sink, and we get ready for a military-like assault on Whole Foods.

Every sponsorship deal is different. My deal with Whole Foods is that we have a $15,000 credit with them, which basically means we can shop till we drop.

"Listen up, everyone, here are your assignments," Mary Sous says. She has taken the supply list that we devised last night and divided it up among us.

Phil has barely come to a rolling stop before Suzi, Mary, and I leap out of the Winnebago and split in three different directions. It's 9:00 a.m. and the clock is ticking. We run amok through the aisles, filling our shopping carts like contestants on those old game shows who get to keep everything they can get their hands on during a 10-minute shopping spree. Little old ladies scramble for cover as we tear through the store. An hour later, shoppers stop and stare as the four of us form a human chain on the sidewalk and unload five overflowing carts of groceries with the speed of a well-oiled machine.

"Done!" Mary Sous shouts. I look at my watch: 10:15 a.m. We have 15 minutes before we have to pop the pass-through window on the Toastermobile and start feeding hungry shoppers. We're sampling two recipes from my book: Shrimp on the Barbie (see page 202) and Spears of Fire (a.k.a. grilled asparagus; see page 137).

As I'm buttoning up my logo-splashed chef's jacket, I'm trying to remember if I reminded Mary to defrost the shrimp and Suzi to unearth another container of dry rub from the storage bin below the RV. And did Phil refill the propane tank for the grill? With each of these questions answered (no, but Mary Sous can run water over them, yes, there's another stash, and, "Shit, I don't know but it's too late now," respectively), I drag the Weber grill out and fire it up on the tarmac. By some miracle, there is enough propane left to get us through the event.

While I grill the asparagus, Mary Sous tosses the shrimp with the dry rub and squirts some cilantro sour cream sauce into a ramekin. Before you can say "Come get your free samples," a gaggle of curious onlookers has begun to gather.

The small crowd attracts more people. A couple of them seem to know who I think I am, but the rest have been attracted by the sight of a giant toaster parked incongruously amidst the SUVs. I circulate among them, tongs in one hand and a plate of shrimp and napkins in the other, putting them down only to sign books. After an hour, Suzi comes over and whispers, "Five-minute warning." Mary Sous has already started to clean up, and I remember that we have a bookstore appearance on the other side of town in just over an hour.

"Thanks so much," I say to the mother toting her kids who has just bought three books for future Christmas gifts. "I gotta roll."

As Phil negotiates his way through the morning traffic, I get to work.

Five phone calls and two cups of Earl Grey tea later, Suzi calls out a five-minute warning from the shotgun seat. Damn. I haven't even checked my email yet. Balancing awkwardly on one leg as the vehicle sways, I slide the other leg into a clean pair of chef pants, grabbing my electric razor with my left hand and cupping the phone between my right ear and shoulder.

In a parking lot the size of a football field, a man is gesturing toward the Toastermobile, guiding us in the direction of a row of orange cones in front of a mammoth Barnes & Noble.

We've arrived late, but because Mary Sous prepped for this event at the last one, we're able to fire up the grill and start serving shrimp and asparagus faster than most people can microwave a burrito. I serve up a few platters of shrimp, sign some books, and then head inside the bookstore for an interview with a local, alternative weekly newspaper. My chef's jacket is splattered with oil and my eyelids are heavy. Luckily, the air-conditioned coolness of the store revives my energy and the reporter—who, refreshingly, has read my book *and* cooked a meal from it—is a blast to talk to.

All too soon, Suzi appears and politely interrupts us. "Bob, sorry, but we need to go."

En route to the dinner party location, we root through the freshly stocked RV refrigerator and I make everyone sandwiches for lunch.

It's 3:45 when we roll up to the suburban house owned by one of the B&G execs. In short order, the crew and I become a mobile dinner party commando squad. We unfold two long tables onto the front lawn, pop the pass-through window, off-load the grill, and start prepping.

In just under three hours, 18 guests—including B&G bigwigs, some of their VIP customers, four journalists, and a distant cousin of mine—will descend upon us. I am, I realize, a little nervous. This is Mary Sous's first dinner party. And though she has been cooking with me for other sorts of events during the three days since she parachuted into the tour, dinners are different. Timing, details, and organization all need to be precision-perfect for the evening to come off well. Forget one pan in the oven, or one step in a recipe, and the meal (and possibly my reputation, depending on the guests) could be, um . . . toast.

Tonight's menu reads like a best-of selection from my book. I'm starting with my familiar shrimp on you-know-who, and grilled asparagus. The entrée is halibut baked in a brown paper lunch bag topped with papaya salsa (see page 26), and roasted purple Peruvian potatoes finished with olive oil and sea salt. It's followed by a cheese course—served on a giant mousetrap that I made out of wood and copper tubing from Home Depot. And for dessert I'm making my Faux Fries (see page 212)—strips of pound cake that are baked until they resemble french fries, then served in McDonald's french-fry containers. I get a kick out of people's puzzled reactions when they get served french fries for dessert, and the looks of wonder as they take their first bites.

Individually, each course is simple. But prepping and cooking all this from scratch in three hours for 18 people, with a brand new sous chef to boot? It's doable, but not easy—just like everything on this tour.

Mary Sous and I quickly fall into our cooking groove. The controlled frenzy of chopping, slicing, grating, grilling, and whisking that follows has the intensity of an emergency room during a full moon. And just like a real toaster, this larger-than-life version becomes red-hot on the inside. With the oven cranked to 475°F, the gas range fired up, and no air-conditioning in the sweltering Florida heat, it is hot enough in here to roast both of us alive, right along with the halibut.

Before we know it, it's 6:45. I duck into the RV to towel off and change into a clean chef's jacket, leaving Mary Sous to finish the prep. Guests begin to arrive, and Mary Sous emerges from the Toastermobile with a tray of Vouvray. The asparagus comes off the grill, and the shrimp are piled around Barbie's plastic torso. People are digging the shrimp. So far, so good.

One by one, the courses are plated and served. Throughout the night, I slip into the kitchen at strategic moments to test doneness, plate the food, and, most importantly, make sure Mary Sous is getting it right. Then I go out and work the crowd. Somehow it all comes together. The stove doesn't run out of propane, the fish is perfectly cooked, the selection of stinky cheeses blows everyone away, and my Faux Fries survive the humidity.

With the guests in a food-and-wine-induced trance, I walk out to the front of the home to check on Mary Sous as she cleans up from the madness. On the quiet, palm tree–lined street, a vintage Bowie track is spilling out from the Toastermobile into the darkness. Mary Sous is grooving to the music, feet tapping on the diamond-pattern steel floor as she starts to put a dent in the mound of dishes. I step inside and we high-five mutual congratulations on a job well done. A wave of relief floods over me. The day, which started in the distant mists of 5:00 a.m., is almost done. The morning's TV appearance seems like a lifetime ago.

Mary Sous rides the wave with me. Suddenly we are infected by the opening guitar riff of Bowie's "Suffragette City" and we both start bouncing around the Toastermobile to the beat. All the manic intensity of the day pours out as pure motion energy. Guests trickling out from the party pause and gaze in astonishment at the sight of two sweat-drenched, food-stained cooks in a giant toaster rockin' out like crazed 15-year-olds in a mosh pit, rupturing the nighttime silence of the suburban street.

During a pause between songs, I suddenly realize I'm exhausted and that every ounce of energy I possess has been depleted. Working as fast as we can, we finish washing the dishes, haul out the trash, put away the pots and pans, scrub the sinks, wipe down and polish the counters and walls, sweep the floor, secure any objects that might spill or roll, latch the drawers, extinguish the lights, and jump into the RV.

Phil has already hitched the RV up to the Toastermobile. As soon as we slam the door behind us, he pulls out. It feels kind of like a hit-and-run job from a wacky 70s comedy: a bank heist with our Winnebago-Toastermobile starring as the unlikely getaway vehicle.

"Go! Go! Go!" Suzi yells, as though the fuzz were hot on our heels, and we lumber toward the interstate.

We have a book signing tomorrow at noon, in Atlanta, 500 miles away. In a motor home towing 5,000 pounds of stainless steel, that takes about 11 hours, which means we have virtually no time buffer. What slave-driving nut agreed to book these two events so damn close together? Shit, that was me.

My eyelids keep trying to close, even though I haven't sat down yet, and my body feels like it's been put through the wringer. Phil drives, country tunes softly playing on the radio to keep him awake, while Suzi reclines in the front seat and Mary stretches out on the dinette table, which converts to a flat bed. In two minutes she is fast asleep, despite the lurching vehicle. I don't know how she does it.

The back of the Winnebago also doubles as a rolling wine cellar. I survey the cache and select a bottle of B&G Châteauneuf-du-Pape—one of the fringe benefits of having a wine company as a sponsor. As king of the rolling fiefdom, I get the real bed in the back of the RV. But with each bump in the Florida asphalt, the mattress bounces wildly. And every pothole and crack in the pavement is accentuated exponentially by the springs. I grit my teeth and try to doze off, but it's like trying to sleep on the back of a bucking bronco.

Sometime around 5 a.m. Phil pulls off at a Motel 6 for a couple hours of rest. With the vehicle stationary, I finally fall into a deep slumber. Even the rush of interstate traffic whooshing by fails to disturb me.

I dream that I am waiting in the wings of a morning show. I'm on the air in three minutes and suddenly, in a sickening, stomach-turning moment, I realize that I've forgotten to prep any of the ingredients for the demo. "Next up, we've got the Surreal Gourmet, who is going to show us an unusual way to make flambéed pineapple," the talk show host announces. Mary Sous is beside me, panicked, shaking my shoulder and saying "Bob, I can't believe we forgot to prep for this! Bob! Bob! . . ." And suddenly in real life, I'm awake and Mary Sous, already dressed for the new day, is shaking my shoulder and saying, "Bob, we are at the bookstore. Get up."

I square my shoulders and stumble out of the RV into the parking lot, blinking in the bright sunlight that reflects off the Toastermobile. Almost as if we had planned it this way, we are right on time. I smile as I'm introduced to the store manager, then I bound into the Toastermobile to prep yet another round of shrimp. It's showtime again, and if you can't stand the heat . . .

"If you are going through hell, keep going."
—Sir Winston Churchill

Over the course of three months, we traveled all the miles, cooked all the meals, and shook all the hands I had fantasized about nine months earlier. My journey was covered by *People* magazine and CNN. I appeared on countless local morning shows, nightly news programs, and even QVC. And my book was featured in the food and entertainment sections of local papers across the US and Canada. I wouldn't be telling the whole story if I didn't also acknowledge that there were plenty of book signings along the route where the only people waiting for us were the in-store staff masquerading as customers to help save face.

Along the way, we toured the Clinton White House and had a rare glimpse of the wine cellar, cooked for the assembly line workers at the Airstream factory, and met countless kindred spirits. I burned through three drivers, two sous chefs, and a whole lot of cash—crossing the finish line $60,000 over budget.

There is no question that I bit off more than I could chew. And it nearly killed me. But in the end—despite how tough it all was—I enjoyed every morsel.

brown-bagged halibut with papaya salsa

This is the kamikaze dinner party entrée I served on the Toastermobile tour. It combines dead-easy preparation, healthy ingredients, fresh tropical flavors, colorful presentation, and the joy of wowing your guests—all in one simple dish. Try it. A brilliant dinner is practically in the bag.

brown-bagged halibut

2 tablespoons (30 mL) peanut or olive oil (or a lesser amount of olive oil spray)
Two 6-ounce (175 g) halibut fillets
1 teaspoon (5 mL) freshly ground black pepper
1½ tablespoons (22.5 mL) peeled and freshly grated ginger
1 tablespoon (15 mL) soy sauce
1 tablespoon (15 mL) freshly squeezed lime juice

2 lunch-size brown paper bags

Preheat oven to 425°F (220°C).

Drizzle 1 tablespoon (15 mL) of oil over the outside of each bag and rub it with your hand until all surfaces of the bag have absorbed the oil. (If you are using oil spray, spray bags generously, then rub oil into paper.)

Rinse fillets, then pat dry. Pepper both sides.

In a small bowl, mix ginger, soy sauce, and lime juice.

Set bags on their side and place one fillet inside each bag. Then, using a tablespoon, spoon the ginger-soy-lime mixture over the fillets by reaching into each bag. Force excess air from the bags, roll up the open ends, and tightly crimp to seal them shut.

Bake on a cookie sheet for approximately 10 minutes, or until fish is cooked throughout and no longer opaque. If necessary, open a bag to check doneness. Cooking time will vary slightly depending on the thickness of the fillet.

To serve, slit open the bags, peel back the paper and spoon Papaya Salsa overtop fish.

papaya salsa

1 ripe papaya (ripe = slightly soft to the touch), skinned, seeded, then diced into ¼-inch
     (6 mm) cubes. If papayas are unavailable, replace with a mango or peach.
2 green onions, trimmed then diced
¼ cup (60 mL) chopped fresh mint or cilantro (stems discarded)
2 tablespoons (30 mL) freshly squeezed lime juice
2 tablespoons (30 mL) finely chopped red bell pepper or red cabbage (for color)
1 jalapeño chili, seeds and membranes discarded, minced

Combine all ingredients in a bowl and mix thoroughly with a fork. Reserve.

yield 2 servings halibut and 1 cup (250 mL) salsa **uncommon goods** 2 lunch-size brown paper bags **safety note** Recently issues have been raised about the safety of cooking in some brown paper bags. If you are at all concerned, replace with aluminum foil bags (which do not require oiling). **level of difficulty** As easy as preparing a brown-bagged lunch. **active prep time** 25 minutes **cooking time** 10 minutes **advance work** Fish can be prepped in bag a couple of hours in advance. Salsa can be made earlier in the day. **music to bag by** James Brown, *20 All-Time Greatest Hits!* Yes, Papa's got a brand new bag. **liquid assets** Viognier. This varietal, which tastes like a cross between Chardonnay and Gewürztraminer, is much easier to drink than it is to pronounce. The ripe tropical fruit notes in the wine pair naturally with the ginger and papaya flavors of the fish.

getting set up

prepping yourself and your kitchen

A fully loaded kitchen isn't going to improve your culinary prowess any more than a new tennis racket will propel you onto the professional circuit. The most important tools in any kitchen are a functional work space, a will to cook, and a palate that understands the inherent taste sensations of fresh ingredients. It's about attitude, not money. Fifty cents' worth of fresh garlic, ginger, shallots, chilies, or lime juice can instantly transform any ho-hum dish into a techno-flavored party in your mouth. By developing the confidence to create bold combinations, you can throw together a meal worthy of impressing a date, or simply improve the pleasure quotient of the food you scarf down in front of the tube.

From there, you can develop the instincts you need to cook for larger groups. The formula for fulfillment in the world of Surreal Gourmet dinner partydom is simple: create an inviting environment, purchase the freshest available ingredients, master a few dishes, download a spirited playlist, invite a wild-card guest, and train your friends to arrive with fine wine. Follow my suggestions when they feel right, or just wing it. Missing ingredients, mismatched utensils, and haphazard kitchen gaffes will all melt into comic irrelevance amid the smoke and sizzle of a little spontaneity.

DIY kitchen feng shui

ONE OF THE MOST EFFICIENT WAYS to reduce the amount of time you spend in your kitchen, and make the time you do spend there more pleasurable, is to create a permanent, ergonomically friendly prep station that is always in a ready state of alert. Here are a few simple, easily implemented, inexpensive modifications that will help create a fluid and efficient work space that will work with you, not against you.

designate Transforming a small kitchen (and sometimes even a big kitchen) into an efficient work space often requires a radical rethink. I am not talking about a full-scale renovation, just a reconfiguration of whatever you've got to work with. The first step is selecting the most efficient work area in your kitchen and designating it as the center of your prep universe. Ideally, this will be a space where you can work comfortably and chat with anyone who may keep you company. In small kitchens, making room for an adequate prep area often requires some triage and the repositioning of inconsequential objects that take up prime real estate. Secondary appliances like the breadmaker you last used six months ago and oversize storage jars are common offenders. Rethink *everything* with fresh eyes. Do you really need that decorative wooden block that houses eight knives, six of which you rarely use? Move the offending items onto overhead shelves, under counters, or into storage—whatever it takes. Once you have selected an area for your prep station, entrench it by installing a solid cutting board as a permanent fixture. If your counter surface is slippery or uneven, place a rubber mat or a dishtowel underneath it.

illuminate Your cutting area should be as well lit as a stage. If you have track lighting, position one or more lamps to illuminate the work space, ideally in such a way that your body won't cast a shadow over the cutting surface. (If your head does get in the way of the light, try bouncing the light beam off the wall in front of you.) If there is a cabinet over your work space, stick an easy-to-install fluorescent light underneath it.

situate Keep your top 10 most-used kitchen tools (tongs, whisks, spatulas, wooden spoons . . .) and your knives within arm's reach of your workstation. Magnets, hooks, and empty olive oil or tomato cans are helpful organizing tools. The best five bucks I ever invested in my kitchen was a galvanized aluminum hook that I bought at my local hardware store and installed at waist level—I hang my omnipresent dishtowel from it. If you install a similar setup in your prep area, you will be able to keep your hands clean without looking down or interrupting the rhythm of your prep work because you'll instinctively know where the towel is.

Notwithstanding my edict on small appliances, if you have the counter space, locate the ones you use frequently where they are the most accessible—this will make you more inclined to use them. Since I decided to keep my panini maker on the countertop, I've used it infinitely more often (and now I'm contemplating annexing my neglected toaster to the hinterlands of my kitchen).

relocate The majority of kitchen garbage containers are hidden under a lid behind a cupboard door, under the sink, or in a corner several paces from the prep station. Getting to the bin and lifting the lid with an armful of vegetable cuttings can require the dexterity of a Cirque du Soleil contortionist. If you can't permanently locate your garbage beside your

prep station, conserve your energy by setting an uncovered trash bucket or bag at your feet beside your prep station each time you start cooking. If you keep a separate bucket for compostable kitchen scraps, move it beside your garbage.

vibe-rate Music makes a cook happy. And a happy disposition is an ingredient you can really taste (just ask any Buddhist). Instead of upgrading to a new multi-setting 40-horsepower blender, spend your money on a pair of wireless bookshelf speakers. Without any carpet or upholstered furniture to muffle the sound, virtually any speaker will add some rock 'n' roll hoochie koo to the small confines of a kitchen.

smart shopping

I AM OBSESSED WITH FLAVOR—the kind of big, bold flavor that knocks you off your feet, then body slams you to the mat before you know what's hit you. That kind of flavor comes from great ingredients. And great ingredients are a result of smart shopping. No matter where you shop, if you buy ingredients at the top of the flavor and freshness chain, they will heighten the flavor quotient of everything you make, and do a lot of the hard work for you.

In conventional grocery stores, inspired shopping is one part resourcefulness and one part sheer determination. Leave your inhibitions behind and scrutinize for freshness by prodding and smelling. At farmers' markets, many of the vendors are the actual farmers themselves, so ask questions. When they detect even a flicker of interest in their produce, they usually become a fountain of information on everything from selection and storage to recipes.

A few of the ingredients called for in this book are quite specific and are not available in every grocery store. Sometimes you have to venture beyond the familiar to get your hands on specialty items and ethnic delicacies. Turn your journey into an education by asking for samples and recommendations for products you may be unaware of. If you keep an open and inquisitive mind, the dividends for your trek will manifest themselves in the form of higher-quality ingredients and lower prices. If you live in a small town where certain ethnic ingredients (i.e., Asian wonton wrappers) are unavailable, pick some up on your next visit to the big city and freeze them, or march into your local Chinese restaurant and ask to buy a few. When all else fails, order ingredients over the Web. With Google and FedEx, the world is your oyster Rockefeller.

If I had a nickel for every time someone whinged that they didn't have the time to throw together a simple dinner from scratch, I'd have two-fifty . . . maybe even three bucks by now. The truth is that with a little forethought and creativity, you can enjoy life-affirming meals in less time than it takes to make mac 'n' cheese from the box—literally—and without breaking the bank. Talent in the kitchen isn't even a prerequisite. If your basic culinary skill set is at, say, the Lindsay Lohan level, these shopping tips will improve the quality of your chow, and leave you with plenty of time to do whatever it is that's keeping you so damn busy.

get fresh   Befriend the butcher and the produce people and they will become your personal sous chefs. The butcher can give you special cuts, repackage portions, trim meats, and fillet fish—all of which will reduce your prep work. The produce people are under strict orders to blow out their existing stock before replenishing the fruit and veggie displays with the latest shipments. If the Swiss chard is limp, chances are there's a pristine bunch behind the swinging doors that is yours for the asking. Sure, a surly face will meet you at the door, but once they have read your determination they will usually acquiesce. On the surface they may seem put off by the extra work, but deep down they will respect you for recognizing the difference in quality.

feather your nest   The key to spontaneous cooking is a well-stocked artillery of nonperishables. The more staples you have on hand, the more options you have when you get home tired and hungry. Here's your pantry primer:

☞ olive oil (a cheap one for basic uses and a fancy one for drizzling)
☞ toasted sesame oil
☞ hot chili oil
☞ safflower oil
☞ balsamic vinegar
☞ rice wine vinegar
☞ soy sauce
☞ Tabasco sauce

- Worcestershire sauce
- Dijon mustard
- kalamata olives
- anchovies
- canned black beans
- canned garbanzo beans
- capers
- dried oregano
- dried thyme
- ground cumin
- ground cayenne pepper
- all-purpose flour
- panko (Japanese breadcrumbs)
- dried pasta
- rice
- sugar
- kosher salt and sea salt
- honey (which, I have discovered, tastes sweeter when served from a honey bear)

(For more on what I consider my favorite nonessential but life-enhancing staples, see page 249.)

the art of presentation

"The first taste is with the eyes."
—attributed to Sophocles

I TEND TO FRET over the appearance of my food even when I am eating alone. And chefs in high-end contemporary restaurants have elevated presentation to such an art that some-times they use more ingredients to dress the plates than they do for the actual food itself. You don't need to go to such extremes, but a little attention to detail can make a big impression. For the uninitiated, here's a quick tutorial to help you unleash the artist within.

conceptualize After making the decision about what to serve, take a moment to let your mind's eye fast-forward to each of the finished courses.

- Think about the colors of the main food elements as well as everything else you are planning to put on the plate. Then ask yourself: does this dish have the potential to be visually stimulating, or will it be a mishmash of beige on beige? To add color contrast, consider substituting vegetables or introducing another component such as a colorful

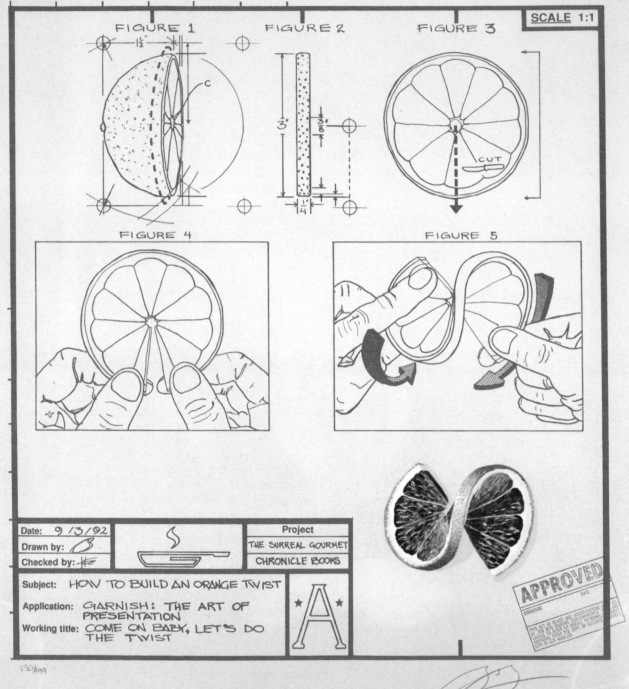

FIGURE 1 FIGURE 2 FIGURE 3 SCALE 1:1

FIGURE 4 FIGURE 5

CUT

Date: 9/3/92		Project
Drawn by:		THE SURREAL GOURMET
Checked by:		CHRONICLE BOOKS

Subject: HOW TO BUILD AN ORANGE TWIST

Application: GARNISH: THE ART OF PRESENTATION

Working title: COME ON BABY, LET'S DO THE TWIST

★ A ★

130/009

sauce that can act as a foil for the other colors on the plate. Or choose a different-colored plate or a different garnish that does a better job of accenting the food.

☞ Think about the shapes and sizes of the food, and how you plan to position it on the plate. For example, when serving carrots, will they look best sliced lengthwise, width-wise, or on an angle? Or should you cook them whole, nouvelle style, with a bit of the green top left intact?

compose Treat your plate like a canvas.

☞ Determine which part of the plate will sit directly in front of the diner.

☞ Use color, texture, size, and shape to balance the composition.

☞ Create symmetrical and circular patterns, which are the easiest and usually the most satisfying to the eye. To expand your repertoire, take note of the presentation tricks used by chefs in the restaurants you patronize or the magazines you read. Most of what you see can be easily duplicated.

☞ Think like a food stylist. "Cheat" your presentation by bringing the star ingredients to the top of any dish that is a mélange of ingredients. This is especially relevant for pastas, salads, and stews.

☞ Check to see that all of the food is at its radiant best before serving. A last-minute glaze of lemon, butter, oil, or sauce can add extra sparkle to the dish.

☞ Wipe any sauce or drippings from the edge of the plate with a clean, damp towel.

☞ Add the garnish last and use it as a final flourish to provide balance for your composition.

☞ Apply many of these same tenets to family-style platters.

garnish A generation ago, a garnish was a piece of parsley and a fancy garnish was a piece of watercress. Today's chefs have elevated garnishing to a high form of art. Don't be intimidated. Even Jeff Koons had to start somewhere.

☞ Choose garnishes that accentuate the other colors on the plate.

☞ Select garnishes that are derived from ingredients in the meal (i.e., use basil leaves as a garnish for a pesto dish or fennel tops for a Pernod-flavored dish). Avoid the tempta-tion of using attractive-looking-yet-incompatible garnishes that could contaminate your flavors if they sneak onto a fork (as they are wont to do).

☞ Add contrasting or exotic elements such as edible flowers or colorful fruits (i.e., cross-sections of kiwis, blood oranges, or star fruits—Nature's gift to garnish-challenged cooks).

☞ Take advantage of the wide borders of oversize plates by framing the meal with a dusting of herbs or spices such as ground pepper, paprika, and/or finely chopped chives. For desserts, use sweet accents such as a dusting of chocolate powder or icing sugar, or drizzles of honey or fruit sauces.

the art of the dinner party

DINNER PARTIES CAN BE INTIMIDATING on so many levels. And for good reason. Unless you have a fetish for napkin rings or silverware, don't sweat the small stuff. I am all about the dinner party anchored by a joie de vivre, a few memorable dishes, and a bounty of freely flowing wine. To get with the program, forget everything your mother taught you about proper dinner party etiquette, grab your corkscrew, and *laissez les bons temps rouler*.

the scene of the crime

THERE IS NO SUCH THING as an inadequate kitchen or dining space for a dinner party. Parties that are forced to battle the limitations of kitchenettes, cramped eating quarters, insufficient furniture, [insert your usual excuse here], etc., tend to generate a communal sense of accomplishment as the host and guests bond while surmounting the obvious challenges. Some of the best dinner parties I've ever attended have taken place in cramped apartments, on rooftops, and with improvised utensils.

Transforming an unaccommodating setting into a workable one requires unlocking your brain from the confines of conventional thinking. If the dining room is too small, move the dining-room table into the living room. If you only have two chairs, get rid of them altogether, seat your guests on the floor, and serve Japanese food and sake. Too hot? Eat outside. Too buggy? Make it a safari party and build a tent from mosquito netting. If all else fails, borrow someone else's place. Some people are happy to lend out their home or apartment as a way of meeting people from outside their immediate circle (with the provisos that they are invited and the cleanup is taken care of).

Oven space and refrigerator space are valuable commodities when cooking for large groups. And limited counter space is the most common hindrance. Sometimes a little ingenuity is required to convert unusable space into a functional prepping and plating area. Cover the sink with a cutting board, turn a cookie sheet upside down and place it over the stovetop, and clear the decks of any appliances or items that are not required for the meal (i.e., the juicer, toaster, breadmaker, coffeemaker, coffee grinder, kettle, cookie jar—I think you get the picture).

guest dynamics

THINK OF YOUR DINNER PARTY as a chess game. To play, you need an assortment of kings, queens, bishops, knights, and pawns (prawns help, too). It's the chemistry between the pieces that makes the evening work. Too many of one piece, regardless of its rank, will never lead to checkmate.

☞ In addition to an eclectic mix of personalities, I like to invite one outspoken, controversial "ringer" whom I can count on to invigorate the conversation. I make a mental note of these types when I meet them at other events, and I lure them to my parties with the promise of fine food. Do the same, or bait your own hook.

☞ It's also fun to introduce "new blood" to a party at the point when the energy level typically wanes. If you have invited friends who can't attend dinner because of previous commitments, turn a negative into a positive by asking them to come late, for dessert or after-dinner drinks. Their arrival will inject your party with a surge of vitality.

☞ Ever since Martians stole my memory, I have dreamed about eliminating the following introductory pleasantry: "Do you two know each other?" Instead of risking embarrassing your guests, risk being redundant by introducing them to one another as though it is for the first time. Then, help to establish a conversational flow by incorporating common ground into your introduction (i.e., work, places they've lived, common friends, children, etc.).

☞ Who is seated by whom can stimulate conversation and enrich the natural energy of the evening. Sometimes, a little meddling is required to help it along. Keep the silent types out of the far corners, and away from the Ringer (to avoid their being trampled). Split up couples and good friends who may get too insular, and pair those who have the potential to complement—and hopefully to compliment—one another. If you have a seating plan in mind and don't want your guests to deviate from the plan, put a place card at each setting. If place cards seem too formal, spell out the names or initials with alphabet cereal or letters clipped from a newspaper. If you want to avoid place cards altogether but still want to exert some control, do it subtly ("Quincy, why don't you sit here . . .").

☞ If you find it challenging to avoid being cornered at your own party, here's a savvy trick I am told the Queen of England uses: before your party, establish an inconspicuous distress signal with your significant other or a designated accomplice. The key is to keep it really simple. Something like scratching your right earlobe. When you are being held captive in an extended discourse with no polite avenue of escape, catch your accomplice's eye. Then discreetly scratch your earlobe or whatever, signaling an immediate need to be called away due to "an impending culinary disaster." Just remember, keep it subtle—or you will look like a third base coach giving the bunt signal.

☞ If only half of the invited guests show up, reconfigure everything to suit the number of people in attendance. Remove excess settings and chairs, fold up the table flaps, and reduce the volume of food accordingly. If no one shows up, look out the window for signs of imminent natural disasters. If none are in sight, check the date in your daybook. If it's the correct day, ask yourself: "Am I a bad person?" If the answer is no, divide the dinner up into single portions, freeze them, and pour yourself a glass of champagne to drown your sorrows.

☞ If twice the number of invited guests show up, consider yourself a social and culinary god and pour yourself a glass of champagne to celebrate. Then halve the portion sizes, double the amount of garnish, and rechristen the meal "California cuisine."

atmospheric conditions

ALL OF THE COMPONENTS of the dinner party setting operate in concert to create a particular atmosphere that affects you on an intangible level, like pheromones. It's always exciting to arrive at a dinner party and have your "Spidey sense" tell you that a special evening is in store. That vibe emanates from the combination of scents, lighting, music, environment, guests—and most importantly—the aura of the host. (With so much emphasis placed on preparing the meal, it is important to remember that guests feed off your energy as much as your food.) If a little attention is focused on each of these details, they will project an overall impression that can become contagious.

how to throw a dinner party—and enjoy it too

- Select a menu that can be prepared entirely in advance.
- Avoid inviting anyone for whom you need to remain on your best behavior (i.e., a potential employer or prospective mother-in-law).
- Invite friends you want to spend time with into the inner sanctum of your kitchen.
- Drink enough—but not too much.
- Seat yourself next to your favorite guest.
- Lure someone to stick around for the "postmortem" after the other guests have left.

☞ The right mix of music can enliven a party. The wrong mix can be distracting and downright annoying. And a complete lack of music can be deadening. Sometimes, the only difference between "right" and "wrong" is timing, tempo, or volume. A little forethought and a few playlist options can make all the difference.

☞ Candlelight can cast a calming and flattering glow on your home and guests, and can transform the simplest meal into an occasion. If you are feeling extravagant, light the entire space in which you are entertaining with candles. IKEA specials and inexpensive paraffin utility candles work beautifully—and produce the exact same light as the infinitely more expensive hand-dipped variety.

menu management

IT'S OK TO BE SELFISH. The first thing to consider when selecting a menu is where *you* want to spend the majority of the evening. If you have an open concept kitchen and confidently think of cooking as a spectator sport, then a menu requiring preparation after the guests arrive is no problemo. If you are culinarily challenged or like to mingle with your guests before dinner, a selection of dishes that can be completed entirely in advance is more practical. A mix of the two, weighted slightly toward pre-prep, is usually a safe choice. And if you are a certified dinner party phobic attempting to overcome your anxieties, select recipes that can be prepared earlier in the day or even the day before (i.e., soups and curries, which actually improve with time). That will free you up to face your demons head-on.

discriminate Great food fuels the party spirit. But that doesn't mean one needs to spend the entire day cooking or break the bank to finance the groceries. I use one fundamental rule when determining what to serve: make a minimal number of dishes, but make each one memorable. A nibble or two (like olives, nuts, or a dip), an appy, and an entrée served with fresh bread should be enough to satiate any guest's hunger, as well as their palate. If you really want to go crazy, toss in a salad. Pastas, risottos, roasted chickens, and stews are a few examples of simple and inexpensive dishes that you can find foolproof recipes for, then enhance with your own signature twist. The Italians have a term for this type of cooking: they call it *cucina povera*.

visualize Visualization and preplanning are the keys to a smooth-flowing, disaster-free dinner party. After you have selected a mix of recipes with which you feel comfortable, take some time to focus on the number of guests, the menu, your cooking arsenal, and your prep space. Picture yourself preparing and serving the dishes you intend to make. If the act of visualizing all of this causes butterflies in your stomach, simplify the menu and/or change the mix to include more recipes that can be prepped in advance.

Next, imagine that it's 15 minutes before showtime. Which dishes and which finishing steps do you see as problematic? Adjust your game plan accordingly. To avoid missing a crucial step that you discover after it is too late to remedy it, create a "critical path" by establishing the sequence in which each dish needs to be started, refreshed, or reheated. I always scribble out a running order and stick it on the refrigerator.

accommodate These days it's virtually impossible to randomly select a half dozen allergy-free, politically like-minded, calorie-unconscious North Americans who will eat anything placed in front of them. To add to the unpredictability, more people are becoming "flexitarians"—which, roughly translated, means that if the bacon-wrapped penguin on a bed of endangered water lilies is tempting enough, they'll eat it in a heartbeat.

There are three ways of dealing with your dinner guests' quirks. The first is to pick your friends wisely. The second is to poll them before you set the menu. Do this by attaching a "quirk questionnaire" with your invitation. Be forewarned: Pandora kept her box locked for a reason. A more manageable solution is to take the following preventative action:

☞ Avoid the most common offenders (i.e., veal, rabbit . . .).

☞ Where possible, add verboten ingredients or allergy-inducers (i.e., nuts, dairy products . . .) at the last minute. This provides your guests with the opportunity to catch you in the kitchen and ask for their portions to be dished out before the problematic or offending ingredient is added.

☞ Prepare extra salad and vegetables so that there will be enough to create meal-size portions for anyone unable, or unwilling, to eat the main course.

portion patrol

GREAT FOOD IS HARD TO RESIST. However, indulging in too much of it in one sitting snaps you out of your culinary orgasm and sends you spiraling into a state of discomfort. We've all been there. It's that I'm-never-going-to-eat-again feeling.

The prime cause of overeating is the lag time between the moment you swallow and the moment your stomach signals to your brain that food has arrived. That's why at a typical Thanksgiving dinner many diners are well into their second helping of turkey, stuffing, and mashed potatoes before their stomachs recognize their predicament and send an urgent text to their brains. Unfortunately, at this point, there's no turning back. And to make matters worse, pumpkin pie is the brain's favorite dessert.

The following tips for policing yourself and your guests are painless examples of how a little vigilance can help you quit while you are ahead:

- Minimize the quantity of predinner nibbles. Hungry guests will scarf down appetizers as fast as they are put in front of them—and then look at you with puppy-dog eyes, hoping for another bone. As flattering as this may seem, don't cave. Sure, it's tough love, but your guests' stomachs will thank you for it later.

- Pace the meal. Instead of serving courses one on top of the other, leave some breathing space—and hope it is filled with stimulating conversation.

- Serve memorable food, not memorable portions. Use garnishes and artful presentation to make less appear like more on the plate.

Remember, you are not being stingy with your food, you are being generous with your concern. Übereaters are always welcome to come back for seconds (after a designated waiting period).

booze rules

- Before-dinner cocktails and out-of-the-ordinary concoctions can add an extra dimension to any meal. But be wary of the well-mixed martini paradox: a cleverly concocted contemporary vodka-based martini can taste like it contains no alcohol at all, despite the fact that it is almost 100 percent alcohol. Not surprisingly, guests can knock back a few of these deceptively yummy elixirs before noticing the effects—at which point it is often too late.

- Despite the traditional guidelines for serving red and white wine, the only thing you can really count on is that your guests will always drink more of the color you have less of.

- If wine is the prime liquid being consumed, a safe range is from half a bottle up to a full bottle of wine per person. To be safe, err on the high side—leftover uncorked wines are rarely orphaned for long.

- If you sense that a guest has gone out of his or her way to bring a special wine, acknowledge the gift in the kindest way possible—by opening it.

- Even if you have an enviable wine cellar, there is always one person who would prefer a beer. Plan accordingly, or you will find them chugging your '61 Lafite Rothschild when what they secretly wanted, but were too intimidated to ask for, was a Bud.

tips for keeping inebriated guests from driving home

- Invite and encourage designated drivers.
- Collect keys at the front door as guests enter.
- Create a cab fare insurance fund (i.e., everyone contributes a few bucks as they enter).
- Provide a comfortable sleeping space, and promise an enticing breakfast and lots of aspirin.
- Keep the number of a safe-ride service or a friendly taxi company on speed dial.
- Match those who need rides at the end of the night with those who can drive.
- Body tackle.

☞ My own exhaustive morning-after research has determined that people tend to continue drinking in the home-stretch as a reflex action rather than from a desire to consume more alcohol. Toward the end of the evening, present a second option by setting out abundant bottles of sparkling mineral water.

(For more musings on wine, see page 224.)

dishing it out

PLATING A LARGE NUMBER OF MEALS quickly is a challenge, even for professional chefs. Before you start to assemble each plate:

☞ Predetermine how you want your finished dish to look (see The Art of Presentation, page 33).

☞ Retaste. Whereas some dishes improve with time, others go flat when prepared too far in advance. If necessary, "refresh" them with salt, pepper, lemon juice, and/or a generous portion of the same herbs that were originally used to flavor the dish.

☞ Make space to set out all your dishes.

☞ Confirm that all of the guests are accounted for.

☞ Have all of the food elements and garnishes ready to be dished out.

☞ Have the appropriate serving utensils on standby.

☞ Set the plates (ideally warmed; see sidebar on following page) out on the available counter space.

☞ Execute any last-minute steps, such as tossing the salad.

☞ Make up the first plate according to the blueprint in your mind. Then, with the help of one or two guests-cum-sous-chefs, knock out the rest as quickly as possible, assembly line–style.

☞ If, due to limited counter space, you are assembling the plates in small batches, verify that you have enough of everything to complete the remaining dishes before sending any finished dishes out to the dining area. On more than one occasion, I've had to go back and poach bits from several plates to make up a final serving or two. That's doable in the kitchen, but somewhat embarrassing once the plates have been served.

☞ Wipe any drippings from around the edges of the plates with a clean dish towel and check that garnishes are in place before allowing each dish to leave the kitchen.

wing it!

ALTHOUGH SOMETHING IS ALWAYS BOUND to go wrong at a party, don't let any catastrophe short of a mass food poisoning spoil the evening. Be prepared. But if that doesn't work, be prepared to wing it. If you are missing ingredients, try borrowing from an accommodating neighbor (knock on their door with a glass of wine or piece of dessert in hand to offer in return). If you ruin the entrée or run out of food, call a restaurant, a pizza joint, or a grocery store that delivers. If that's not an option, order the goods with a credit card and send a taxi to pick them up.

temperature tips

SERVE HOT FOOD HOT. If you have prepared some elements of the meal ahead of time, reheat them to their appropriate temperatures just before serving.

DON'T SERVE COLD FOOD TOO COLD. Remove cold food from the fridge 15 to 30 minutes before serving so that the chill doesn't mask the flavors.

NEVER SERVE HOT FOOD ON COLD PLATES. Warm all dinner plates, serving plates, and bowls in the oven at 200°F (95°C) for 10 minutes. If the oven is full, warm them under hot tap water, then stack them and place a dishtowel overtop to retain the heat.

it ain't over till it's over

WHEN GUESTS VOLUNTEER TO CLEAR THE TABLE, they are usually being sincere. When they offer to stick around to clean up and help do the dishes, what they are really saying is: "Wow, what a disaster, but I'm tired and I have an early meeting tomorrow." Interpret such offers as you wish, but if you let them off the hook, take solace in knowing you are paving the way to a guilt-free exit from their next soirée.

After the party has wound down and the guests have departed, one of the evening's most pleasurable moments awaits the host and their chosen confidante. I call it the party "postmortem." Pull a stool up by the sink, sit your coconspirator down beside you, and let fly while you do the dishes. Even the worst culinary crises, political gaffes, and social faux pas can be laughed at when scrutinized under the postmortem microscope. Bad hair, bad dress, bad manners, and bad dates are all fair game once the guests are out of earshot. If this seems uncharitable, don't fret; it's a safe bet they are critiquing your social graces and your food on the drive home. By the time the gossiping has reached a feverish pitch, you should have plowed through all of the dishes and the party will be officially wrapped.

appy hour

cocktail bites

The cocktail bites showcased in this section are designed to scream with flavor and defy their size. Any one of them is guaranteed to deify the person who brings it to a party. A couple of them can jump-start a fabulous soirée and create a halo effect around anything else you serve. And five or six will work beautifully for a dinner party or a cocktail party as a complete menu. In any configuration, they are definitely showstoppers and conversation starters.

chinese sno-cones

Chinese chicken salad is an Asian-inspired California creation consisting of grilled chicken, crisp lettuce, deep-fried wonton strips, and nuts—all tossed in a tangy ginger vinaigrette. Everybody's version is different. With most, the crispy wontons put the crunch in the salad. I've inverted the concept and reengineered mine so that the salad is in the crispy, crunchy wonton.

1 large single boneless, skinless chicken breast
Salt
1¼ cups (310 mL) peanut oil, divided
Sixteen 3½-inch (9 cm) square wonton wrappers (4 are backups)
1 tablespoon (15 mL) peeled and finely grated fresh ginger
1 tablespoon (15 mL) freshly squeezed lime juice
1 tablespoon (15 mL) honey
1 teaspoon (5 mL) Dijon mustard
1 teaspoon (5 mL) soy sauce
1 teaspoon (5 mL) seasoned rice vinegar
1 cup (250 mL) sliced and finely diced napa cabbage (about ¼ head)
½ cup (125 mL) sliced and finely diced radicchio (about ¼ head)
½ cup (125 mL) coarsely chopped roasted unsalted cashews
⅓ cup (80 mL) canned mandarin slices, chopped
¼ cup (60 mL) finely chopped fresh cilantro (stems discarded)
2 green onions, finely sliced
Chili pepper flakes

Twelve 4- or 6-ounce (125 mL or 185 mL) paper cones

Season chicken breast with salt. In a small sauté pan over medium heat, add 1 tablespoon (15 mL) peanut oil. Cover and cook chicken for 6 to 8 minutes per side, or until no pink remains. Reserve.

Preheat oven to 350°F (180°C).

In a small bowl, set out 1 cup (250 mL) peanut oil along with a small pastry brush. On a baking sheet, set out 12 paper cones.

Trim 12 wonton wrappers according to diagram on page 255. Generously brush both sides of each wrapper with peanut oil. Wrap one wrapper around each cone and press seam together. Twist the bottom around itself. Bake for 7 minutes, or until golden brown and crispy. When wonton cones cool, twist them off the paper cones. Reserve.

Dice chicken into ¼-inch (6 mm) cubes. Reserve.

(continued . . .)

(. . . continued)

In a large bowl, whisk together 3 tablespoons (45 mL) peanut oil, ginger, lime juice, honey, Dijon, soy sauce, and rice vinegar. Just before serving, add chicken along with cabbage, radicchio, cashews, mandarins, cilantro, and green onions. Toss thoroughly and season to taste with salt and chili pepper flakes. Spoon into wonton cones just before serving. Serve cones in shot glasses, or make your own cone holder.

yield 12 cones **uncommon goods** Cone-shaped paper cups (available by office water coolers and at restaurant supply stores); wonton wrappers (available in Asian groceries and the refrigerated section of many grocery stores) **level of difficulty** Wonton cups require the pattern-making skills and dexterity of an amateur seamstress. **active prep time** 1½ hours **shortcuts** Skip the wonton cups and serve chicken salad in paper cones or mini paper cups; start with a precooked chicken breast. **advance work** Wonton cones, ginger dressing, and the slicing and dicing of salad ingredients can be done up to a day in advance. Toss just before serving. **music to cook by** Carl Douglas, "Kung Fu Fighting." A song that puts the "kitsch" back in the kitchen. **liquid assets** A Kabinett Riesling from Germany, or a new-world off-dry Riesling, should supply the perfect balance of crispness and fruitiness for the vibrant flavors of the salad and the zingy dressing.

ahi sno-cones

The pleasing size and satisfying crunch of the wonton cones that contain my Chinese chicken salad (see page 48) garner many kudos. After *Surreal Gourmet Bites* came out, I started using them to serve all sorts of fillings. Tuna tartare was a natural fit. After I added the whimsical toppings, ahi sno-cones quickly became another one of my staple party treats.

1 cup (250 mL) peanut oil (for brushing wonton wrappers)
Sixteen 3½-inch (9 cm) square wonton wrappers (4 are backups)
10 ounces (300 g) sushi-quality ahi tuna, finely diced
1 ripe, fragrant peach, papaya, or mango; peeled, pitted, and diced in ¼-inch (6 mm) cubes
3 green onions, finely sliced
10 fresh mint leaves, finely chopped
Zest of 1 lime
2 tablespoons (30 mL) sesame seeds, toasted
¼ cup (60 mL) soy sauce
1 teaspoon (5 mL) wasabi paste
2 teaspoons (10 mL) toasted sesame oil
1 teaspoon (5 mL) freshly grated ginger
1 tablespoon (15 mL) *yuzu* or freshly squeezed lime juice
1 ripe avocado, pitted and peeled
2 tablespoons (30 mL) freshly squeezed lemon juice
Salt and freshly ground black pepper
Pinch of cayenne pepper
12 teeny-weeny cherry tomatoes

Twelve 4- or 6-ounce (125 mL or 185 mL) paper cones

Preheat oven to 350°F (180°C).

In a small bowl, set out peanut oil along with a small pastry brush. On a baking sheet, set out paper cones.

Trim 12 wonton wrappers according to diagram on page 255. Generously brush both sides of each wrapper with peanut oil. Wrap one wrapper around each cone and press seam together. Twist the bottom around itself. Bake for 7 minutes, or until golden brown and crispy. When wonton cones cool, twist them off the paper cones. Reserve.

In a medium bowl, combine tuna, peach, green onion, mint, zest, and sesame seeds. Reserve.

In a small bowl, combine soy, wasabi, sesame oil, ginger, and yuzu. Taste the dressing and adjust if necessary. Reserve.

(continued . . .)

(. . . continued)

In a mini food processor, or in a bowl using a whisk, purée the avocado and lemon juice until it is supersmooth. Season to taste with salt, pepper, and cayenne. Transfer to a small piping bag or a small resealable bag with the corner clipped. Reserve.

to finish and serve

Add about half of the dressing to tuna mixture. Toss and add more as required to dress, but not drench. Taste and add a pinch of salt if necessary. Spoon tuna into cones. Top with a dollop of avocado purée and a cherry tomato. Serve cones in shot glasses, or make your own cone holder.

yield 12 cones uncommon goods Cone-shaped paper cups (available by office water coolers and at restaurant supply stores); wonton wrappers (available in Asian groceries and the refrigerated section of many grocery stores); sushi-quality tuna (available at most groceries with a fresh fish department—always explain that you are eating it raw) level of difficulty Wonton cups require the pattern-making skills and dexterity of an amateur seamstress. active prep time 1½ hours shortcuts Skip the wonton cups and serve tartare in paper cones or mini paper cups. advance work Wonton cones, dressing, and the slicing and dicing of tartare ingredients can be done earlier in the day. Toss just before serving. music to cook by Kazu Matsui, *Sign of the Snow Crane*. A great collection of traditional Japanese music played on a bamboo flute known as a shakuhachi. liquid assets Nigori sake. This roughly filtered, cloudy sake (served chilled) has a mild tropical flavor that will meld perfectly with the ginger and wasabi—and expand your sake horizons.

coconut shrimp lollypops

Developing this recipe was the beginning of my love affair with small bites. The harmonic convergence of sweet fresh coconut, succulent shrimp, tropical dipping sauce, and a Trader Vic's–style presentation was an instant crowd-pleaser. Like a trained seal, I love to perform this trick and bask in the applause the lollypops incite. They are a bit involved, but mastering them is a lot easier than learning how to balance a ball on your nose.

coconut shrimp lollypops

1 coconut (first-timers should buy a spare coconut)

½ cup (125 mL) beer (if required)

1 cup (250 mL) all-purpose flour

1 egg

1 teaspoon (5 mL) cayenne pepper

¾ teaspoon (4 mL) baking powder

½ teaspoon (2 mL) salt

12 raw medium shrimp (21/25 count—that's 21 to 25 to a pound/500 g),
   peeled and deveined

3–5 cups (750 mL–1.25 L) peanut oil or vegetable oil (for frying)

1 wedge of watermelon (for presentation)

Twelve 6-inch (15 cm) bamboo skewers

With the coconut and a medium bowl in hand, go find yourself a concrete step. Break the coconut in half by banging the center (along the equator) of the coconut repeatedly on the edge of the step (see diagram page 255). Split the coconut over the bowl and salvage some of the water if possible. Reserve the smaller half of the coconut. Bang the larger half on the concrete to break it into smaller pieces.

Back in your kitchen, use a table knife to separate the coconut meat in the small pieces from the shell. Then use a vegetable peeler or paring knife to remove the brown skin from the meat. Using the medium section of your grater, shred 2 cups (500 mL) of coconut. Reserve in a shallow bowl.

Pour coconut water into a measuring cup and, if necessary, top it off with beer until you have ¾ cup (185 mL) of liquid. Reserve. (If you are using store-bought shredded coconut—and consequently do not have any coconut water—replace this mixture with ¾ cup/185 mL of beer.)

In a large bowl, combine the flour, coconut water/beer mixture, egg, cayenne, baking powder, and salt. Beat until it is smooth. Add a bit more flour or beer, if necessary, so that the batter has the consistency of thick pancake batter. Reserve.

(continued . . .)

(. . . continued)

Use a paper towel to pat dry the shrimp. Tightly wrap each shrimp like a pinwheel (with the tail end of the shrimp on the outside), then place 1 shrimp on the end of each 6-inch (15 cm) bamboo skewer (see diagram page 255). Reserve in the refrigerator.

Before frying, see Fear of Frying (page 246).

Pour oil into a small, tall pot until it is 3 inches (8 cm) deep. Heat oil until it reaches 350°F (177°C).

While oil is heating, dip each shrimp in the batter, then pat it down in the coconut shreds so that the entire lollypop is covered in coconut shreds. Transfer to a plate.

When oil is ready, submerge 4 shrimp at a time into the oil. Don't worry if the skewers go into the oil. Fry for approximately 2 minutes, or until coconut is golden brown. Rotate once or twice. Transfer finished lollypops to a paper towel.

Skim any wayward coconut shreds from the oil. Adjust heat, wait until oil returns to 350°F (177°C), and continue with next batch. Stick skewers in a watermelon wedge and serve the dipping sauce in the reserved coconut half.

apricot-ginger dipping sauce

¾ cup (185 mL) apricot jam
1 jalapeño chili, seeds and membranes discarded, minced
2 tablespoons (30 mL) seasoned rice vinegar or freshly squeezed lime juice
1 tablespoon (15 mL) freshly grated ginger
1 tablespoon (15 mL) Dijon mustard

Place all dipping sauce ingredients in a blender or food processor. Purée. Reserve.

yield 12 lollypops **uncommon goods** 6-inch (15 cm) bamboo skewers; a whole coconut **level of difficulty** Like learning how to line dance. If you attempt all of the steps together, it can be intimidating the first time around. But if you tackle each of the individual steps of this recipe one at a time, they are a cinch to master. **active prep time** 1 hour **cooking time** 15 minutes **shortcuts** Skip the fresh coconut. Use store-bought unsweetened, shredded coconut in place of the fresh coconut; beer in place of the coconut water; and a small decorative bowl for the dipping sauce in place of the coconut shell. **advance work** Coconut can be grated, shrimp can be skewered, and the dipping sauce and batter can be made earlier in the day. The shrimp can be battered and dredged a couple of hours before serving and refrigerated on a plate. That just leaves the deep-frying to be done at showtime. **music to cook by** Harry Nilsson, *Everybody's Talkin'*. "She put de lime in de coconut, drink 'em bot' toge-der . . ." **liquid assets** A crisp, semi-dry German or Alsace Riesling has the acidity to cut through the deep-fried coconut, and the fruitiness to temper the heat of the dipping sauce.

chicken popsicles

When I do cooking demonstrations, I often start with these savory popsicles. Within minutes, an off-the-rack chicken breast and three bowls of basic breading ingredients morph into flavorful, succulent bites. (To make these pleasing pops even more accessible, I adapted the original recipe to work with simple boneless chicken breasts instead of chicken tenders.) Add a one-cent bamboo skewer and stick 'em into a pineapple or watermelon wedge, and with a minimal amount of effort, you've created a fantabulous grown-up treat.

2 boneless, skinless chicken breasts
Salt and freshly ground black pepper
⅔ cup (160 mL) all-purpose flour
2 eggs
⅔ cup (160 mL) panko or coarse breadcrumbs
⅓ cup (80 mL) (about 1½ ounces/45 g) freshly grated Parmigiano Reggiano
2 tablespoons (30 ml) dried oregano
1 tablespoon (15 mL) dried thyme
2 tablespoons (30 mL) butter
1 tablespoon (15 mL) olive oil
3 tablespoons (45 mL) freshly squeezed lemon juice
1 pineapple or watermelon wedge (for presentation)

Twelve to sixteen 6-inch (15 cm) bamboo skewers

Remove the chicken tenders (the separate piece of the meat that runs under the breast) and place the chicken breasts shiny side up. Use a tenderizing mallet or the bottom of a pot to flatten the breasts and tenders to ¼-inch (6 mm) thickness. Cut the flattened chicken into 1-inch(ish) (2.5 cm-ish) squares. Season with salt and pepper.

Set out 3 medium bowls. Place flour in one; crack the eggs into the second and beat them. In the third, add panko, Parmigiano Reggiano, oregano, and thyme. Line the 3 bowls in a row.

Toss about a third of the chicken in flour until well covered, then swirl it in egg until well soaked, and finally, roll it in panko mixture until completely covered. Transfer to a plate and repeat process with remaining chicken.

In a frying pan, over medium-high heat, melt butter and add oil. When butter begins to sizzle, add chicken. Cook for approximately 3 minutes on the first side, or until bottom is golden brown. Turn once and cook for approximately 2 more minutes, or until the second side is golden brown and the nuggets are cooked throughout. To test for doneness, make a small incision in a sacrificial nugget. If any pink remains, return chicken to heat for another minute or two.

(continued . . .)

(. . . continued)

Transfer your future pops to a plate. Remove pan from heat and immediately add lemon juice. Stir for 10 to 15 seconds to loosen up brown bits and let the lemon juice reduce by half. Drizzle a few drops over each tender and season with salt. Insert a skewer through the end of each chicken nugget, then stick skewers in pineapple.

yield 12–16 popsicles **uncommon goods** 6-inch (15 cm) bamboo skewers **level of difficulty** Think Shake'n Bake. **active prep time** 20 minutes **cooking time** 10 minutes **shortcuts** Buy Italian-style breadcrumbs that are seasoned with herbs and cheese. **advance work** Chicken can be breaded earlier in the day and refrigerated on a plate. **multiplicity** For each additional batch of popsicles, make an additional half recipe of the breadcrumb mixture. **music to cook by** Ry Cooder, *Chicken Skin Music*. Any excuse to put on a Ry Cooder album is a good excuse. **liquid assets** A crisp Italian Soave will cut through the rich crust and match the acidity of the lemon glaze.

gaucho snacks

My great-great-uncle was an honest-to-goodness gaucho in Argentina. Cattle ranchers employed him to herd their cattle across the Argentinean plains to the coastal markets where the cows were sold and shipped overseas. At night during these rugged treks, the gauchos would set up camp, build a big wood fire, and roast a whole cow over the open pit (after all, when you're moving entire herds, who's counting?). A traditional fiery sauce was concocted and basted on the meat as it turned. Then the seared meat was carved directly from the spit. My grandfather adapted the method and grilled rib-eye steaks over the coals of the furnace under the men's clothing store he owned in Montreal. My dad continued the family tradition in our backyard. In his retirement years, he rechristened himself "Gaucho Jack" and began bottling the sauce.

By the time I started shooting *The Surreal Gourmet*, Gaucho Jack was in his 80s. He came on the show, and with a twinkle in his eye, he divulged the coveted family recipe. (He also boxed me into a corner of my Toastermobile—literally—much to the amusement of the crew.)

To prepare for the episode, I created my own version of Chimichurri Sauce, another Argentinean staple that is used both as a marinade and a condiment. I make mine in a blender, and it takes about five minutes to prepare from start to finish. Despite the fact that my dad didn't sanction my messing with family history, the chimichurri was a huge hit on set and has since become a staple sauce in my own repertoire. With a nod to Gaucho Jack, I now use it as an instant upgrade for any simply grilled piece of steak, chicken, or fish. I'm convinced that in the world of grilling, it's the best five minutes you can spend. If the old gaucho were still around, I know that he would secretly approve.

NOTE: The grilling sauce doesn't taste so good on its own (which thwarted my dad's marketing efforts). The magic all happens in the grilling process as the water in the sauce evaporates and the salt and cayenne bind to the proteins in the steak.

(continued . . .)

(. . . continued)

gaucho steak

3 tablespoons (45 mL) sea salt or kosher salt
1 tablespoon (15 mL) cayenne pepper
Two 1-pound (500 g) New York strip or rib-eye steaks,* ideally 1¼ inches (3 cm) thick
1 sourdough baguette, sliced in ¼-inch-thick (6 mm) slices

Preheat grill to high direct heat (see page 247). In a jar, mix salt, cayenne, and 1 cup (250 mL) hot water. Seal and shake until salt dissolves.

Place steaks on grill and immediately drizzle a tablespoon (15 mL) of grilling sauce overtop. Repeat after turning steaks. For extra spicy steaks, baste an additional time as they cook. Grill steaks to your desired degree of doneness (approximately 5 minutes per side for medium-rare if you are using New York strip, and 2 minutes per side for skirt steak). Remove the steaks from the grill, cover with aluminum foil, and let rest for 5 minutes.

To serve, cut steaks into ¼-inch-thick (6 mm) slices. Set slices on bread and top with Chimichurri Sauce. For individual servings of steak, chicken, or fish, serve sauce at the table.

chimichurri sauce

4 cups (1 L) fresh Italian parsley (stems discarded)
5 tablespoons (75 mL) olive or vegetable oil
2 tablespoons (30 mL) freshly squeezed lemon juice
3–5 cloves garlic, minced
1 medium shallot, minced, or 2 tablespoons (30 mL) minced onion
1½ tablespoons (22.5 mL) sherry vinegar or red wine vinegar
¼–½ teaspoon (1–2 mL) chili pepper flakes
½ teaspoon (2 mL) salt
½ teaspoon (2 mL) freshly ground black pepper

Place all ingredients in a food processor or blender and pulse for about 30 seconds until very well chopped, but not quite puréed. Reserve.

yield 16 steak bites, 1 cup (250 mL) Chimichurri Sauce **level of difficulty** Requires basic caveman skills. **active prep time** 20 minutes **cooking time** 20 minutes **shortcuts** Skip the Chimichurri Sauce. Even without it, this is a killer bite for steak lovers. **advance work** Chimichurri Sauce can be made up to a day in advance. With minimal sacrifice, steak can be grilled a few hours earlier and served at room temperature. Slice just before serving. **revelation** On a recent pilgrimage to Argentina, I learned that my interpretation is brighter, fresher, and greener than those commonly served in local restaurants. **music to cook by** Astor Piazzolla, *Tango: Zero Hour*. The greatest innovator in tango's history. Beautiful, passionate, and fiery. **liquid assets** An Argentinean Malbec, big and rough, will wrangle the bold flavors of this dish.

* I've recently started using skirt steak. It is about half the price of a New York strip. Though it doesn't share the same succulent mouthfeel, it has a much more intense and satisfying meaty flavor. If you choose to use it, always slice it against the grain.

cocktail dates

In their unadorned state, Medjool dates are intense candy bombs that explode in your mouth with sweetness and richness. But stuff them with the nuttiness of Parmigiano Reggiano, wrap them in the smoky saltiness of bacon, and bake them, and they turn into molten balls of decadence that will blow your mind.

12 large dried Medjool dates
4-ounce (125 g) chunk Parmigiano Reggiano
6 slices bacon, cut in half widthwise

12 wooden toothpicks

Preheat oven to 350°F (180°C).

Use a paring knife to make a lengthwise slit in each date. Splay open the dates and remove the pits. Reserve dates.

Using your sharpest knife, cut Parmigiano Reggiano into sticks that are 1 × ¼ × ¼ inch (2.5 cm × 6 mm × 6 mm).

Fill the pit cavity of each date with a piece of cheese. Close the dates around the cheese and press to seal.

Wrap each date with a piece of bacon and set on a baking sheet, seam side down. Skewer with a toothpick to hold bacon in place.

Bake for approximately 20 minutes, or until bacon is crispy. Caution: These flavor bombs are like molten lava when they come out of the oven. Let cool for a few minutes before serving.

yield 12 bites **uncommon goods** Medjool dates (usually available in Middle Eastern stores and specialty food stores) **adventure club** Use a cob-smoked bacon or another type of specialty bacon. **full disclosure** The instructions in *Surreal Gourmet Bites* for this recipe involved a ridiculously elaborate technique for extracting the pits from the dates with the tip of a bamboo skewer. Shortly after the book was published, I figured out the painfully obvious method I have outlined above. I offer a deep, heartfelt apology to anyone who squandered precious minutes of their lives attempting to follow my needlessly complicated and time-consuming instructions. **level of difficulty** If you have ever rolled a joint (or seen someone roll a joint . . . on TV), you are fully qualified. **active prep time** 15 minutes (now 50 percent faster!) **inactive cooking time** 20 minutes **shortcuts** Buy pitted dates. **advance work** Dates can be stuffed and wrapped as much as 24 hours in advance. **music to cook by** Various artists, *Cocktail Mix, Vol. 4: Soundtracks with a Twist.* A swingin' extravaganza of 60s movie music, including tunes by Bacharach, Mancini, and Morricone. **liquid assets** The over-the-top pruney qualities of an Italian Amarone are a good match for the naturally concentrated sugars in the dates.

tuna fish 'n' chips

Consider the blue corn tortilla chip. Along with blue potatoes and blueberries, they are part of a rarefied club of naturally blue foods. Despite this astounding fact, we eat blue chips cavalierly by the handful without a passing thought. But put these triangular marvels in the spotlight and they shine as the perfect vehicle for a melt-in-your-mouth slice of cumin-crusted tuna.

avocado relish

1 ripe-but-still-firm avocado, cut in ¼-inch (6 mm) cubes
½ cup (125 mL) frozen corn kernels, thawed
¼ cup (60 mL) finely chopped fresh cilantro (stems discarded)
¼ cup (60 mL) diced red onion
2 tablespoons (30 mL) freshly squeezed lime juice
Salt and freshly ground black pepper

In a medium bowl, combine all the relish ingredients and toss gently. Reserve.

tuna

12 ounces (375 g) sushi-quality ahi or albacore tuna, 1 inch (2.5 cm) thick
1 teaspoon (5 mL) freshly ground black pepper
1 teaspoon (5 mL) ground cumin
½ teaspoon (2 mL) ground coriander
½ teaspoon (2 mL) salt
¼ teaspoon (1 mL) cayenne pepper
1 tablespoon (15 mL) canola oil
12 cosmetically perfect blue corn tortilla chips

Cut tuna into triangular strips, 1¼ inches (3 cm) per side (see diagram page 255). In a small bowl, combine pepper, cumin, coriander, salt, and cayenne. Rub spice mixture generously on all 3 long sides of the tuna.

Heat a nonstick pan over high heat. When pan is smoking hot, add canola oil. Wait 10 seconds, then add tuna. Sear for 30 seconds per side, or until fish is cooked on the outside but still rare in the center. Transfer to a plate. Slice into ½-inch-thick (1 cm) triangles just before serving.

To assemble, line up tortilla chips. Top with a dollop of Avocado Relish and a slice of tuna.

yield 12 bites **level of difficulty** The only challenge is staying focused for the 1½ minutes that the tuna is searing. If necessary, double up on your Ritalin. **active prep time** 30 minutes **shortcuts** Skip the relish and put a slice of avocado under the tuna. **advance work** Tuna can be seared earlier in the day and served at room temperature. Slice just before serving. Relish can be made earlier in the day. **music to cook by** Danny Elfman and friends, *Big Fish* soundtrack. Elfman's score to Tim Burton's film runs the stylistic gamut from haunting and mellow to dramatic and orchestral. **liquid assets** The chips, avocado relish, and cumin all beg for a Mexican beer or a margarita.

bang-bang drummettes

Buffalo chicken wings ordered "suicide" on the spice scale used to be one of my guilty pleasures. But now, my palate craves more complexity. My bang-bang marinade packs plenty of heat but also delivers multiple layers of sweetness and spice fused with Asian and Caribbean flavors. And by using just the meatiest section of the wing, there is less fight and more bite.

18 chicken wing "drummettes"
6 cloves garlic, minced
¼ cup (60 mL) pineapple juice
¼ cup (60 mL) soy sauce
2 tablespoons (30 mL) toasted sesame oil
2 tablespoons (30 mL) olive oil
2 tablespoons (30 mL) freshly squeezed lime juice
2 tablespoons (30 mL) honey
1 tablespoon (15 mL) ground cinnamon
1 habañero or Scotch bonnet chili, seeds discarded, minced; or 1 teaspoon (5 mL) habañero
    or Scotch bonnet hot sauce

If wings come attached to middle and/or tip sections, cut away at the joint and save for soup. Using a paring knife, cut around the bone just below the knuckle, at the skinny end of each drummette. Slice through the meat and tendon (see diagram page 255). Scrape the meat up toward the fat end of the drummette, creating a ball-like shape at that end. (There is no need to be precise; the cooking process will shrink the meat and complete your artistry.) Trim off the bit of fat at the knuckle. Transfer chicken to a large resealable plastic bag. Reserve.

In a blender, purée remaining ingredients. Transfer marinade to the bag o' chicken, force out air, and seal. Refrigerate for a minimum of 2 hours, but ideally for 6. Massage occasionally.

GRILL METHOD
Preheat grill to medium-high direct heat (see page 247). Grill for 20 minutes, rotating a quarter turn every 5 minutes, or until cooked throughout.

OVEN METHOD
Preheat oven to 450°F (230°C). Bake for 25 minutes, ideally on a wire rack, turning once.

yield 18 wings **uncommon goods** Habañero chili, or habañero sauce **level of difficulty** Like a trip to the hairdresser: a few snips, a little fussing with some product, a bit of time for everything to settle into place—and you're good to go. **active prep time** 25 minutes **inactive prep time** 2–6 hours **inactive cooking time** 25 minutes **shortcuts** Have your butcher trim and prep the wings. **advance work** Drummettes can be prepared and left to marinate up to 24 hours in advance. With minimal sacrifice, they can also be cooked a few hours in advance, then reheated in a 450°F (230°C) oven for 8 minutes. **multiplicity** For each additional batch of drummettes, make an additional half recipe of the marinade. **music to cook by** Mickey Hart, *Global Drum Project*. Hailed as "a danceable, multitextured celebration of rhythm." **liquid assets** A Belgian blond beer has the rich flavor and aroma necessary to tame the habañero and temper the cinnamon.

bee stings

No pigs, cows, or bees were harmed in the making of these tiny taste explosions. But these succulent morsels would not be possible without the precious yield of those creatures' respective foraging, milk producing, and honey making. Thanks to their hard work, this is the least amount of effort you will ever have to expend for the greatest number of accolades.

¼ cup (60 mL) best-available honey
½ tablespoon (7.5 mL) white truffle oil
¼ teaspoon (1 mL) freshly ground black pepper
6-ounce (175 g) block Parmigiano Reggiano

In a small bowl, combine honey, truffle oil, and pepper. Reserve.

Just before serving, use a paring knife to chisel cheese into irregular ½-inch (1 cm) nuggets. Drizzle truffled honey over each nugget.

(To get the most Parmigiano Reggiano for your buck, see page 253).

yield 12 bites **uncommon goods** Truffle oil (available at gourmet food stores for about $10 for a 2-ounce/60 mL bottle) **level of difficulty** You won't work nearly as hard as the bees did. **active prep time** 5 minutes **shortcuts** Skip the truffled honey and drizzle cheese with an aged balsamic vinegar. Or just serve the cheese au naturel. **advance work** Truffled honey can be mixed and Parmigiano can be cut up to a day in advance. Wrap cheese tightly in plastic wrap to keep it from drying out. **multiplicity** You can double the cheese without the need for more truffled honey. **music to cook by** PJ Harvey, *To Bring You My Love*. A scorching disc from an alternative darling who really is the bee's knees. **liquid assets** If you are lucky enough to have—or know someone who has—an old bottle of champagne, you're in for a treat. The toasty, yeasty characteristics of vintage bubbly are an elegant and sophisticated foil for the earthiness of the truffle oil. The rest of us can enjoy an Australian Sémillon blend with honey undertones that will play off the nutty sweetness of the cheese and the drizzle.

cauliflower popcorn

Ever since I adopted this recipe from a good friend and christened it "popcorn," I have become the Pied Piper of cauliflower. Now, everywhere I go I sing its praises. Usually I am met with skepticism when I boast that it's so good even kids devour it. After all, who woulda thunk that cauliflower could actually become addictive? But it's true. With this dead-simple, high-temperature roasting process known as caramelization, basic off-the-rack cauliflower is miraculously transformed into a sweet, lip-smackin' treat that the kids in your world—and even you—won't be able to get enough of.

1 head cauliflower
¼ cup (60 mL) olive oil
1 tablespoon (15 mL) sea salt or kosher salt

1 popcorn container

Preheat oven to 425°F (220°C).

Cut out and discard cauliflower core and thick stems. Trim remaining cauliflower into florets the size of golf balls. In a large bowl, add cauliflower, olive oil, and salt. Toss thoroughly.

Spread cauliflower on a baking sheet (lined with parchment paper, if available, for easy cleanup). Roast for 1 hour, or until much of each floret has become golden brown. (That's the caramelization process converting the dormant natural sugars into sweetness.) The browner the florets, the sweeter they will taste. Turn 3 or 4 times during roasting.

Use crumpled up aluminum foil or paper towels to create a false bottom in your popcorn container, fill it with cauliflower, and serve immediately.

yield 4–6 servings uncommon goods An empty movie theater popcorn container or aluminum Jiffy Pop package. level of difficulty The same as making real popcorn. active prep time 10 minutes inactive cooking time 1 hour shortcuts Buy the precut cauliflower in the lazy-boy section of the produce department. advance work Raw cauliflower can be precut and refrigerated for up to 2 days in an airtight bag or a bowl of water. With minimal sacrifice, cauliflower can be cooked earlier in the day and reheated in a 450°F (230°C) oven for 10 minutes. music to cook by James Brown's *The Popcorn* has Soul Brother #1 servin' up some tasty treats. liquid assets Big buttery Chardonnays may have fallen out of fashion, but they are the perfect pairing for this equally unfashionable cruciferous vegetable.

rings of fire

I was addicted to hot sauces long before I became the Canadian ambassador for Tabasco sauce. Now that I have an unlimited supply, I am so hooked that it would take more than a 12-step program to wean me off the endorphin-inducing heat. I also happen to love crispy onion rings. So for me, bringing the two together is an exercise in efficiency. The result is a winning combination that is a cinch to make. Certified capsicum junkies should add an extra splash of any sauce that has "insanity," "inferno," or "sphincter" in its title.

2 Vidalia or Walla Walla onions or other sweet onions
1½ cups (375 mL) all-purpose flour, divided
2 serrano chilies, minced (plus a couple in reserve)
2 teaspoons (10 mL) sea salt or kosher salt (plus more to season finished rings)
1 teaspoon (5 mL) cayenne pepper
½ teaspoon (2 mL) freshly ground black pepper
1 cup (250 mL) beer
1 tablespoon (15 mL) Tabasco sauce
Peanut oil (for frying)

Before frying, see Fear of Frying (page 246).

Slice onions into ¼-inch (6 mm) slices and separate into rings. Select the 16 largest, most aesthetically pleasing rings.

In a medium bowl, combine 1 cup (250 mL) of the flour, the serranos, 2 teaspoons (10 mL) salt, cayenne, and pepper. Slowly whisk in beer and add Tabasco sauce. The batter should be the consistency of thin pancake batter. Add more flour or beer to adjust if necessary.

In a medium, tall pot, add 3 inches (8 cm) of oil and heat to 350°F (177°C).

In a medium bowl, add remaining ½ cup (125 mL) flour. Toss onion rings in flour to coat. Shake off excess flour.

Dip one onion ring in batter until thoroughly coated, then fry for approximately 2 minutes, or until golden. Turn once during frying. Remove and drain on paper towels. Let cool. Immediately season with salt. Taste. Count to 30, then assess the heat level. Add more of everything hot according to your pain threshold (and that of your guests). Continue frying rings in small batches and serve immediately.

yield Serves 4–6 as a snack or side dish **level of difficulty** The hardest part is figuring out what to do with the other 5 beers. **active prep time** 20 minutes **cooking time** 10 minutes **shortcuts** Skip the serranos and just add more cayenne. Or skip the serranos and the cayenne and just add more Tabasco. **advance work** Batter can be prepared and onions can be sliced earlier in the day. **multiplicity** Existing batter will accommodate another batch of onions. **music to cook by** Johnny Cash, *Ring of Fire: The Best of Johnny Cash*. The taste of love may be sweet, but onion rings will never break your heart and run off with your best friend. **liquid assets** See level of difficulty.

cam 'n' pear quesadillas

On a recent promotional trip to Singapore, I cooked a thank-you dinner for my new BFF at Discovery Travel & Living (the network—now TLC—that carries my shows in Asia). Singapore is a foodie's paradise, and a wide range of amazing culinary experiences are available in "hawker centers" throughout the city. In my quest to serve my hosts something they hadn't experienced before, I dusted off this old chestnut and replaced the pears with fresh local mangoes. To my great relief, the quesadillas disappeared in a heartbeat, which reminded me of how versatile the quesadilla format really is.

1 lime
½ cup (125 mL) sour cream or plain yogurt
¼ teaspoon (1 mL) salt
Four 8-inch (20 cm) flour tortillas
2 jalapeño chilies or 1 serrano chili, seeds and membranes discarded, diced finely
2 ripe pears (any variety), peeled, cored, and cut in ⅛-inch (3 mm) thick slices
6 ounces (175 g) ripe Camembert, cut in ¼-inch (6 mm) slices (rind removal is optional)
1 cup (250 mL) lightly packed fresh cilantro (stems discarded)

Zest the lime, then squeeze it. In a small bowl, combine zest, 1 tablespoon (15 mL) of lime juice, sour cream, and salt until the mixture is smooth. Reserve.

Heat a 10-inch (25 cm) sauté pan or cast-iron skillet over medium heat. Place one tortilla in the dry pan for approximately 40 seconds on each side, or until it just begins to brown. Remove. Repeat with a second tortilla. (If your tortilla expands like a blowfish, poke it with a fork to release the hot air.)

After the second tortilla has browned, leave it in the pan and reduce heat to medium-low. Immediately sprinkle half of the diced chilies onto the tortilla. Cover with half of the pear slices. Place half of the Camembert strips over the pears. Top with half of the cilantro, then cover with second tortilla. Cover the pan with a lid and cook for 2 minutes.

Flip the quesadilla with a spatula, re-cover the pan, and continue cooking for 2 more minutes. (Don't worry if a bit of cheese escapes and begins to sizzle loudly.)

Remove the quesadilla from the pan, let sit for 1 minute, then slice into 8 wedges—just like a pizza. Repeat with the remaining ingredients. Serve with sour cream dipping sauce.

yield Serves 4–6 as an appetizer level of difficulty Somewhere between easy and really easy. adventure club Replace pears with mangoes or papaya. active prep time 15 minutes cooking time 20 minutes shortcuts Go to Taco Bell. advance work All of the slicing and dicing may be done several hours ahead of time. If you slice the pears ahead of time, squeeze the juice of a lime or lemon over them to preserve their color. music Calexico, *Hot Rail.* Southwestern melodies mixed with everything from Morricone-esque soundscapes, Mexican folk songs, and Afro-Peruvian grooves. liquid assets Go new world with a semisweet sparkling Shiraz from Australia.

cucumber shooters

When I was a kid, my mother sent me to a variety of after-school art classes. Over the years I became comfortable working in many mediums—all of which have served to help me create the images and build the objets d'art that have become my signature style (some of which are contained in this book). Here's your opportunity to discover your inner artist and transform the humble field cucumber into a mixed-media art project. All it takes is a couple of common kitchen utensils to turn the ends of the cukes into sculpted vessels, and a few basic ingredients to turn what's left into a zippy and refreshing green gazpacho.

8 cucumbers (the conventional field variety)
¼ cup (60 mL) fresh mint (stems discarded)
1 shallot, minced
1 jalapeño chili, seeds and membranes discarded, minced
2 tablespoons (30 mL) freshly squeezed lime juice
1 clove garlic, minced
¼ cup (60 mL) best-available olive oil
2 tablespoons (30 mL) champagne vinegar or white wine vinegar—or in a pinch,
    red wine vinegar
Salt and freshly ground black pepper

Cut 2½ inches (6 cm) off both ends of each cucumber. Reserve.

Peel middle sections of cucumbers, cut in half lengthwise, and use a spoon to scrape out seeds. Discard seeds.

In a food processor or blender, add the middle sections of the cucumbers along with the mint, shallot, jalapeño, lime juice, and garlic. Purée.

Strain puréed mixture through a fine strainer into a medium bowl. Use a rubber spatula to press out as much juice as possible from the mash. Discard solids. Whisk in oil and vinegar, and season with salt and pepper. Refrigerate the gazpacho for a minimum of 1 hour.

While soup is chilling, take the 12 most aesthetically pleasing cucumber ends and slice ¼ inch (6 mm) off the bottom so that each cucumber stands solidly on its end. Use a zester, paring knife, or vegetable peeler to create designs in the peel. Use a melon baller or a tiny spoon to scoop out the seeds and some of the surrounding cucumber, creating cucumber shot glasses. Stir the gazpacho before serving and pour into the sculpted cups.

yield 12 shooters **uncommon goods** Zester (the kind with a V-shaped groove in it designed to make lemon twists) **level of difficulty** Just like arts and crafts in school: Everyone can do it, some just make it look prettier. **active prep time** 1 hour **inactive prep time** 1 hour **shortcuts** Serve gazpacho in shot glasses or mini paper cups. **advance work** Gazpacho can be made up to 2 days in advance; cucumber cups can be sculpted earlier in the day and refrigerated in plastic wrap. **music to cook by** Patti Smith, *Horses*. An album I originally owned on eight-track. As cool (as a cucumber) today as it was then.

bruschetta threesome

Bruschetta is my go-to predinner nibble. It only takes a few seconds to make, but along with a glass of vino, it will keep ravished dinner guests satiated and buy you valuable time in the kitchen. Needless to say, since so few ingredients are involved, the higher their quality, the better the end result. The following three recipes are all variations on a theme. All of them are so simple that they barely require a recipe. That said, they never fail to please.

bruschetta simplico

4 thick slices rustic country-style or sourdough bread
2 cloves garlic
4–6 tablespoons (60–90 mL) best-available olive oil
Salt and freshly ground black pepper

If you have a panini maker, this is the perfect opportunity to fire it up. If you are grilling, use your fire as a heat source. Otherwise, toast the bread in a toaster, toaster oven, or oven until it is very brown and crispy.

Immediately after toasting bread, rub a garlic clove over the entire surface of one side. Each slice should use up about a quarter to a third of a clove. (Be careful; when the garlic meets the toast's hot surface, it will create fumes that sting your eyes—just like a freshly cut onion.)

Generously drizzle olive oil overtop each slice. Sprinkle with salt and a generous amount of pepper to taste. Slice into 1-inch-wide (2.5 cm) strips and serve immediately.

bruschetta di prosciutto

4 ounces (125 g) prosciutto

Follow all of the steps for Bruschetta Simplico, then top each slice generously with thinly sliced prosciutto di Parma or another air-cured ham, preferably from Europe (see page 253).

bruschetta di pomodoro

2 medium tomatoes, sliced
2 sprigs fresh basil, chiffonaded

Follow all of the steps for Bruschetta Simplico, then top each slice of bread generously with slices of tomato. (Only bother doing this when you can get your hands on really flavorful—and, ideally, colorful—tomatoes.) Top with some basil and an extra sprinkle of salt.

yield Each version makes about 12 nibbles. **level of difficulty** If you can make toast, you can make bruschetta. **active prep time** 10 minutes **shortcuts** Quit while you are ahead with Bruschetta Simplico. **music to cook by** Beth Orton, *Central Reservation*. One of my favorite discs for easing into a dinner party. **liquid assets** Any wine that pairs well with the excitement of arriving guests will work perfectly.

rock-a-molé

Hass avocados, with their bumpy, reptilelike skin, are ubiquitous these days. The oily richness of their flesh requires very little in the way of adornment. In fact, in my humble California-based, guacamole-obsessed opinion, too many ingredients spoil guac, and mayonnaise—don't get me started—downright destroys it. This less-is-more recipe is based on the version I tasted at the Border Grill on one of my first pilgrimages to Los Angeles, many margaritas ago.

2 ripe avocados (ripe = indents easily with the firm press of a finger)
⅓ cup (80 mL) finely chopped fresh cilantro (stems discarded)
2 tablespoons (30 mL) freshly squeezed lemon or lime juice
4 green onions, finely sliced
¼ teaspoon (1 mL) ground dried chipotle or a pinch of cayenne pepper
Salt and freshly ground black pepper (to taste)

Slice avocados in half. Discard skin and pit.

In a medium bowl, combine all ingredients. Blend with a fork, but leave mixture somewhat chunky.

yield Serves 6 as an appetizer level of difficulty *Mas simplico* active prep time 10 minutes advance work Can be made earlier in the day. Cover with plastic wrap pressed directly onto the surface of the guac. music to cook by Los Lobos, *La Pistola y El Corazón* liquid assets Margaritas, *por favor.*

let's get this party started

soups & salads

I think of soup and salad as the inaugural address of a dinner. They set the bar and let everyone know what they can expect for the rest of the evening. Like a well-prepped inaugural speech, soups and salad dressings can be prepared long in advance. This helps to take the pressure off and allows you to focus on your guests, your subsequent courses, and your show-stopping stories.

caesar salad daze (a tutorial)

AFTER PUBLISHING THIS RECIPE IN MY FIRST BOOK, I received hundreds of letters (and now emails) from readers who have mastered the art of making Caesar salad and have been worshipped by their friends. The ultimate compliment came from a waitress at the now-defunct Bamboo Club in Toronto who took me aside and whispered, "Every time I make your Caesar salad for a date, I get laid."

My history with the Caesar goes way back to my college years and an unlikely cooking teacher. Scott Wilson was a practical-joking, golf-loving classmate of mine who put himself through business school by preparing Caesar salads tableside at a swish restaurant in London, Ontario. One Saturday, in my quest to impress a dinner date, I woke him up at two in the afternoon and begged him for a tutorial.

Hundreds of salads and several truckloads of romaine lettuce later, I have fine-tuned the ingredients and learned to articulate the nuances that make or break a Caesar. I am so obsessed with the ritual that when I take my show on the road, I carry my well-worn salad bowl with me in a snare drum case.

Contrary to what anyone in a chef's toque might want you to believe, there are no secret ingredients or difficult techniques to Caesar salad. A quintessential Caesar, with its heady aroma and pungent dressing, requires nothing more than the harmonic convergence of several high-quality ingredients, and a modicum of focus. In order to demystify the process, I have isolated the most essential components. Hopefully your Caesar salad experiences will be as satisfying for you as they were for the waitress at the Bamboo.

the bowl The definitive salad begins with a large, unfinished wooden bowl (i.e., not coated with a shiny lacquer). The rough interior wall of the bowl provides a perfect surface for blending the dressing. (The best bowls are usually bored out of one solid slab of maple). Most restaurant chefs and many home cooks commit a grievous error by using a blender or food processor, which is the wrong tool for the job. These peppy pulverizers overwhip the yolk, giving the dressing an undesirable mayonnaise-like texture.

the grind Once the aforementioned bowl is in hand, facilitating the successful marriage of the ingredients becomes an intensely physical activity worthy of Olympic designation. Use the back side of a soup spoon and a healthy amount of pressure to grind the ingredients in a repetitive circular motion against the interior wall of the bowl. It should take approximately 20 seconds for each new ingredient to blend with the existing ingredients and form a smooth paste.

the cheese Imported Italian Parmigiano Reggiano is one of the most important elements of a great Caesar. A food writer at the *Los Angeles Times* wrote of the cheese, "Once you got a taste of the real stuff—crumbly, earthy, and rich as wine—there's no turning back: everything else is sawdust." After you have added Parmigiano Reggiano to your cooking arsenal, you will be forced to adopt guerilla defense tactics to protect the ungrated cheese. Roaming dinner guests tend to circle the wedge like hungry sharks, and will devour it the second you turn your back to spin-dry the lettuce.

the garlic Use only fresh garlic. Anything less than direct-from-the-bulb—including pre-minced, jarred, pickled, dried, or powdered—is categorically unacceptable. And be wary of elephant garlic—a classic example of more is less.

the lettuce Designer salad greens may be gracing fashionable plates everywhere, but romaine remains the lettuce of choice for Caesars because it wears the heavy dressing so well. If you must substitute, use another hearty lettuce. After washing the lettuce, use a spinner or a towel to remove all water. For maximum crispness, return the lettuce to the refrigerator until just before tossing with the dressing.

the anchovy Don't be intimidated by the sight and taste of anchovies. When blended along with the other ingredients into a paste, the distinctive anchovy taste is virtually unidentifiable. So why use it? Because along with the garlic and Dijon mustard, the anchovy provides the essence of the Caesar dressing, which all of the remaining ingredients serve to enhance. Anchovy paste blends well *and* provides the perfect solution to the old problem of using one anchovy and tossing out the rest of the school.

the croutons Nothing is more anticlimactic than topping a finely tuned Caesar with store-bought croutons that were really intended for turkey stuffing. If you are going to put the effort into making the dressing, go the extra mile and make homemade croutons—they will become the hidden jewels of the salad. If you have more money than time, gourmet-style croutons made by cottage-industry suppliers are a suitable replacement.

the legacy A great Caesar salad should knock you off your chair, then smack you in the head as you struggle to regain your senses. I can appreciate the fact that not everyone likes to wrestle with their salad, but that's why man created bottled dressing. If you elect to reduce the garlic or substitute other ingredients, please don't tell anyone it's my recipe.

chez bob's caesar

Perfect this recipe and the world will beat a path to your door.

¼ teaspoon (1 mL) salt
½ teaspoon (2 mL) coarsely ground black pepper
3 cloves garlic
3 anchovies or 1 heaping teaspoon (5 mL+) anchovy paste
2 teaspoons (10 mL) Dijon mustard
1 egg yolk (see note on using raw eggs page 90)
1 tablespoon (15 mL) freshly squeezed lemon juice
1 teaspoon (5 mL) Worcestershire sauce
5 tablespoons (75 mL) safflower or canola oil
1½ teaspoons (7.5 mL) red wine vinegar
1 large head romaine lettuce, washed and trimmed (if lettuce looks anorexic,
    or is in need of a serious trim, buy 2 heads)
1½ cups (375 mL) croutons (see recipe below)
½ cup (125 mL) (about 2 ounces/60 g) freshly grated Parmigiano Reggiano

Add salt and pepper to the salad bowl (this creates a sandpaper-like base that will make the next steps easier). Add the garlic. Use the tines of a fork to smash up the garlic, then use the back of a soup spoon to grind the garlic against the wall of the bowl until it is thoroughly pulverized. Add the anchovies and once again use the back of the spoon to grind it into a paste. Follow the same procedure, adding the Dijon, egg yolk, lemon juice, and Worcestershire sauce one at a time. Make sure that each ingredient is fully incorporated into the previous ingredients before proceeding. It should take about 20 seconds of muscle power to blend in each new ingredient.

Slowly drizzle in the oil and vinegar, blending well with the spoon as you drizzle.

Tear or slice the lettuce into bite-size pieces and add to bowl. Toss thoroughly with dressing.

Add the croutons and cheese, toss again, and serve immediately.

croutons

3 slices of slightly stale sourdough or rustic country-style bread, cut in ¾-inch (2 cm) cubes
3 tablespoons (45 mL) olive oil

Preheat oven to 350°F (180°C). Place the bread cubes in a large bowl and add olive oil. Toss and squish the bread like a sponge until the oil is evenly absorbed.

Place the croutons on a baking sheet or aluminum foil and bake in the oven for 20 watchful minutes, turning once or twice, or until golden brown. Try not to forget about them in the oven—as I often do.

(continued . . .)

(. . . continued)

notes

☞ Despite my earlier preaching, if you don't have a rough wooden salad bowl, the dressing can be made (with some sacrifice) in a blender or food processor: Add the salt, pepper, garlic, anchovy, Dijon, lemon juice, and Worcestershire. Purée. Add the oil and vinegar, and pulse several times. Then add the egg yolk and pulse a couple of times—just enough to blend it without causing the dressing to turn mayonnaisey.

☞ If you are serving your salad to anyone over 100 years old or to anyone with a compromised immune system, coddle your eggs to diminish the risks involved in using raw egg yolks: Begin with a properly refrigerated egg. Submerge the whole egg in a pot of boiling water for exactly 40 seconds, then remove from the water, crack, and separate the yolk from the white.

☞ I find that the flavor of fancy olive oil overwhelms the dressing, so I use safflower oil. Other light vegetable oils or a light olive oil may be substituted.

☞ The lettuce leaves should be coated, but not soaked, in dressing. To play it safe, remove and reserve one-third of the dressing from the bowl before tossing the salad. Then add back as necessary until your salad is "dressed" appropriately.

yield Serves 4–6 **level of difficulty** Requires the strength of a flyweight arm wrestler and a bit of dedication. **active prep time** 20 minutes **inactive cooking time** 20 minutes **shortcuts** Use pre-washed romaine hearts, store-bought gourmet croutons, and pre-grated Parmigiano Reggiano. **advance work** Dressing, croutons, lettuce, and cheese can be all be prepped earlier in the day. Dressing and lettuce should be refrigerated individually. Assemble and toss salad just before serving. **music to cook by** Jane Siberry, *Bound by the Beauty*. An uplifting album from the ethereal artist I managed during my salad days in the music business.

the beet goes on

Most people are wary of beets, which is not surprising considering the myriad of ways that they can be maligned. For anyone who would eat beets—if *only* they tasted good—there is hope.

Roasting beets at an extremely high temperature for a long period of time intensifies their natural sugars, transforming the humble root into a lip-smackin', almost candylike treat that bears no resemblance to their canned and boiled brethren. But wait, wait, there's more. Beet greens, which are usually discarded like carrot tops, are full of flavor, not to mention vitamins and minerals. In fact, they contain more of these than the beet itself. When sautéed in oil with a bit of garlic, they become as tasty as Swiss chard or spinach.

Admittedly, roasted beets and sautéed beet greens may not seal the deal on their own. But add some goat cheese (even the common variety that is sold in log form) and they become something totally sublime. The earthiness of the cheese is a perfect match for the beet, and its creamy richness complements the wilted greens. When eaten together as either a warm or a room-temperature salad, these three components form a holy trinity that will tempt even the staunchest beet-phobe.

(continued . . .)

(. . . continued)

Be forewarned that the beet goes on. The next day it exits all parts of the system with a harmless splash of red. Think of it as Nature's way of acknowledging your heroic leap of faith.

8 medium-size beets (with tops intact)
4 tablespoons (60 mL) olive oil, divided
1 tablespoon (15 mL) freshly squeezed orange juice
1 teaspoon (5 mL) balsamic vinegar
1 teaspoon (5 mL) freshly squeezed lemon juice
Salt and freshly ground black pepper
2 cloves garlic, minced
2 shallots, diced finely
¼ teaspoon (1 mL) chili pepper flakes
4 ounces (125 g) goat cheese, crumbled or cut in 4 slices

Preheat oven to 450°F (230°C).

Cut off beet greens. Reserve.

Roast beets, skin on, for 75 minutes or until tender to a firm touch. Let cool.

Peel off blackened skin with your hands. Cut beets into ¼-inch-thick (6 mm) slices.

In a medium bowl, blend 2 tablespoons (30 mL) olive oil, orange juice, vinegar, lemon juice, and salt and pepper to taste. Add beets and toss. Reserve.

Thoroughly wash beet greens and shake dry. Strip off any thick stems.

In a sauté pan over medium-high heat, add remaining oil, garlic, shallots, and chili flakes. Sauté for 1 minute. Add beet greens and sauté, covered, for 3 minutes, tossing occasionally, or until greens have wilted. Season with salt and pepper.

To serve, spoon beet greens onto the center of each plate. Mound the beets on the greens and sprinkle or set goat cheese overtop.

yield 4 servings **uncommon goods** Not all beets are sold with their tops intact. Ask your produce person for a bunch that hasn't been trimmed, or replace tops with a bunch of Swiss chard. **adventure club** Use a mix of different-colored beets. **level of difficulty** As easy as baking some potatoes and sautéing some spinach. **active prep time** 20 minutes **inactive cooking time** 75 minutes **short-cuts** Skip the greens. **advance work** Beets can be roasted up to a day in advance and refrigerated in their skins. Greens can be sautéed an hour before serving and served at room temperature. **music to cook by** "The Beat Goes On," Sonny & Cher. La de da de de, la de da de da.

pomegranate mâche-up

Prêt-à-manger baby salad greens (a.k.a. mesclun) were once a pricey gourmet item but are now available in all grocery stores. Some mixes contain as many as a dozen different varieties of baby lettuces and herbs. Like gourmet jelly beans, the flavors blend together when they are all eaten at once. But sample the greens individually, and you will discover their distinctive flavors and textures. A few of my favorite varieties such as baby arugula, frisée, and mâche are now packaged individually.

In this simple-yet-stylish ensemble, the tartness of pomegranate seeds and the sweetness of the maple syrup–infused dressing (which, BTW, is my house dressing) become the perfect accessories for the buttery texture of mâche, creating a very haute couture salad.

4 cups (1 L) mâche (also called lamb's lettuce) or Boston lettuce
¼ cup (60 mL) pomegranate seeds (about ¼ pomegranate)
3 tangerines or oranges, supremed (see page 248)
Salt and freshly ground black pepper

maple-dijon dressing

2 teaspoons (10 mL) Dijon mustard
1 tablespoon (15 mL) maple syrup
2 teaspoons (10 mL) balsamic vinegar
1 teaspoon (5 mL) freshly squeezed lemon juice
3 tablespoons (45 mL) olive oil

For the dressing, whisk together mustard, maple syrup, vinegar, and lemon juice in a small bowl. Slowly drizzle in olive oil, whisking constantly until emulsified.

Just before serving, combine mâche, pomegranate seeds, and tangerine slices in a salad bowl. Add half the dressing and toss gently but thoroughly. Add more dressing as desired, but be careful not to overdress. Season with salt and pepper to taste and serve immediately.

yield 4 servings, ¼ cup (60 mL) dressing **uncommon goods** Pomegranates are available in some grocery stores, Indian stores, and specialty stores. They are generally in season in the fall but are now also being imported at other times of the year from other parts of the world. POM has begun to sell packaged seeds in the refrigerated fruit section of some grocery stores. **adventure club** For a pleasing twist on the dressing, replace olive oil with walnut or hazelnut oil. **level of difficulty** The only hard part is extracting the seeds from the pomegranate without staining the whole kitchen. To contain the mess, fill a large bowl two-thirds full with water and extract the seeds underwater. **active prep time** 25 minutes **shortcuts** Skip the tangerine supreming and use ¼ cup (60 mL) canned mandarin orange segments. **advance work** Pomegranates can be seeded, tangerines supremed, and dressing made earlier in the day. Assemble and toss salad just before serving. **music to cook by** The Beatles, *Love*. Classic Beatles tracks, mixed and mashed.

cirque du salade

In the years that followed the release of my first cookbook, I made annual pilgrimages to Vancouver to visit a free-spirited group of friends. These visits were always synonymous with dinner parties, where I played the ringleader in a culinary circus. On one such memorable trip, the circus traveled to a cottage on Gambier Island, a tiny spit in the Georgia Strait, 30 miles from the nearest food processor. As usual, the kitchen was a cacophony of slicing, dicing, and laughter, accompanied by *The Best of ABBA* playing on an old boom box. There were no matching plates or cloth napkins, no electricity, and no place to run to for last-minute ingredients. But these minor shortcomings were no match for a locally caught coho salmon, four bags of groceries, a case of Prosecco, and a whole lotta love. Nowadays, my then–sous chefs have all cultivated their own areas of culinary expertise and moved on to front their own circuses. My friend Erin (formerly my official Parmigiano grater) was the genesis of this yummy salad.

¼ cup (60 mL) maple syrup
½ cup (125 mL) pecan halves
3 tablespoons (45 mL) olive oil
1 tablespoon (15 mL) balsamic vinegar
1 tablespoon (15 mL) freshly squeezed orange juice
1 large raw beet (ideally golden*), peeled and coarsely grated
1 Fuji apple (or any other hard apple), peeled, cored, and coarsely grated
1 fennel bulb, trimmed and coarsely grated
⅓ cup (80 mL) coarsely chopped fresh mint (stems discarded)
4 ounces (125 g) Stilton (or another blue cheese), crumbled
Salt and freshly ground black pepper

Preheat oven to 350°F (180°C).

Pour maple syrup into a small bowl. Toss nuts in syrup, remove with a slotted spoon, and bake on aluminum foil or a cookie sheet for 10 minutes. The syrup will bubble, and once you take the nuts out of the oven and let them cool, the syrup will solidify. Reserve.

In a large bowl, combine oil, vinegar, and orange juice. Whisk together, then add beet, apple, fennel, mint, Stilton, and nuts. Toss. Season to taste with salt and pepper. Serve immediately.

yield Serves 4 as a hearty salad or a light lunch **level of difficulty** If you can grate a block of cheese, you can make this salad. **active prep time** 25 minutes **shortcuts** Buy candied pecans. **advance work** All ingredients can be prepped earlier in the day. Beet, fennel, apple, and cheese should all be wrapped individually. Toss with dressing just before serving. **music to cook by** Cirque du Soleil, *Alegría*. An amazing album that will waft to the highest peak of your Big Top.

* Golden beets are ideal (if available) because their color does not bleed into the other ingredients.

fire-roasted corn chowda

Nothing beats a cob of farm-fresh corn slathered in butter. But if you are willing to invest a little more time and effort, this chowder recipe will reward you with big corn flavor and complex layers of spice and heat. And best of all, there's no need to floss when you're finished.

8 ears corn, husked
1 red bell pepper
2 tablespoons (30 mL) butter (if pan roasting)
5 cups (1.25 L) chicken stock, divided
2 tablespoons (30 mL) olive oil
4 ounces (125 g) salt pork, pancetta, or thickly
    sliced bacon, diced
6 cloves garlic, finely diced
1 sweet onion (i.e., Maui, Vidalia), finely diced
2 leeks, white and pale green section only, diced
1½ cups (375 mL) finely chopped fresh cilantro
Salt and freshly ground black pepper
¼–½ teaspoon (1–2 mL) ground dried chipotle or a
    pinch of cayenne pepper
1 cup (250 mL) half-and-half cream (optional)
2 tablespoons (30 mL) freshly squeezed lime juice

GRILL METHOD

Preheat grill to medium-high direct heat (see page 247). Roast corn on grill, turning a quarter rotation every 2 minutes or so, until kernels begin to brown. Roast the bell pepper until the skin blackens. Remove corn and bell pepper from the grill and let cool. Cut kernels from the cobs into a bowl. Reserve. Skin and seed the bell pepper, then dice it finely. Reserve.

PAN METHOD

Cut kernels from the cobs, and dice bell pepper. Sauté corn and bell pepper in a large pan with 2 tablespoons (30 mL) of butter for 10 minutes, or until corn begins to brown. Reserve.

In a food processor, purée half the grilled (or sautéed) mixture with half the stock. Reserve. In a stockpot over medium-high heat, add oil and cook pork, garlic, onion, and leeks for approximately 8 minutes, stirring occasionally, until contents begin to brown. To the stockpot, add the puréed corn mixture, remaining stock, remaining corn and bell pepper, and cilantro. Turn up heat until it reaches a boil, then reduce heat and let simmer for 15 minutes. Just before serving, season to taste with salt, pepper, and chipotle. Add cream (if using) and lime juice.

yield 6–8 servings **level of difficulty** Once you have secured farm-fresh corn, the rest is all downhill. **active prep time** 1 hour **inactive cooking time** 15 minutes **advance work** Soup can be made up to 2 days in advance **music to cook by** Jeff Buckley, *Grace*. Buckley's channeling of Leonard Cohen's *Hallelujah* is one of the greatest covers of all time. **liquid assets** A big, luscious white, like a Rhône blend.

cracker jack soup

Every once in a while you've just gotta think outside the box—the Cracker Jack box, that is. This savory-but-sweet peanut soup has its roots in Georgia. I've swapped out several of the traditional ingredients and replaced the cream with coconut milk. The coconut milk adds a layer of rich, exotic flavor that makes this soup a guaranteed home run for kids and adults alike.

1¼ cups (310 mL) shelled peanuts, or 1 cup (250 mL) smooth peanut butter
3 tablespoons (45 mL) peanut or vegetable oil, divided
2 tablespoons (30 mL) butter
1 yellow onion, chopped
1 medium-size yam, peeled and diced in ¼-inch (6 mm) cubes
5 cups (1.25 L) chicken stock
½ cup (125 mL) canned coconut milk (not to be confused with coconut cream)
Salt
Cayenne pepper (optional)
1 tablespoon (15 mL) freshly squeezed lime juice
½ cup (125 mL) Cracker Jacks (for garnish)

In a food processor, add peanuts and 2 tablespoons (30 mL) of the peanut oil. Purée until smooth. Reserve. (If you use peanut butter, omit the 2 tablespoons/30 mL of oil used to blend the peanuts.)

In a large pot over medium heat, add 1 tablespoon (15 mL) peanut oil, butter, onion and yam. Cover and cook for 15 minutes, stirring occasionally. Add chicken stock, coconut milk, and peanut butter. Turn up heat until liquids reach a boil, then reduce heat and simmer for 15 minutes. Let cool slightly, then purée in a blender. Season to taste with salt and cayenne (if using). If sharing with kids, it is a good idea to season theirs separately. To serve, reheat, finish with lime juice, then garnish each bowl with a few Cracker Jacks.

yield 8 servings **uncommon goods** Cracker Jacks are available at some grocery stores, and ballparks everywhere. **level of difficulty** There is little chance of striking out with this recipe. **active prep time** 40 minutes **inactive cooking time** 30 minutes **shortcuts** Choose the peanut butter option. **advance work** Can be made up to 2 days in advance. **music to cook by** Ali Farka Toure, *Savane*. A seminal album of African guitar blues from this Mali-born musician. **liquid assets** A Semillon and Sauvignon Blanc blend is a sweet match for the soup's rich peanut base.

14-carrot soup

A perfect gem of a cold-weather soup. Make it on a chilly weekend afternoon and let the wafting smell of the ginger and nutmeg and the heat of the simmering stockpot warm your entire abode.

14 medium-size carrots (2½ pounds/1.25 kg), peeled
1 medium-size yam or sweet potato
4 stalks celery
3 leeks, white and pale green sections only, sliced in half lengthwise and thoroughly cleaned
6 tablespoons (90 mL) butter
One 3-inch (8 cm) knob of fresh ginger, peeled and coarsely grated
7 cups (1.75 L) chicken or vegetable stock, divided
½ teaspoon (2 mL) freshly grated nutmeg (ideally)
Salt and freshly ground black pepper
1 cup (250 mL) half-and-half cream (optional)

Roughly chop carrots, yam, celery, and leeks.

Heat 2 large sauté pans over medium-high heat. Divide butter, carrots, yam, and celery between the 2 pans. Sauté for 15 minutes, then add leeks and ginger. Continue sautéing for approximately 15 more minutes, or until pan contents begin to brown. Stir occasionally, and moderate heat if necessary to keep contents from blackening.

In a large pot, bring 6 cups (1.5 L) of stock to a boil. Add contents from both of the pans. Cover with a lid, adjust heat if necessary, and simmer for 30 minutes.

Allow soup to cool, then purée two-thirds of the soup in a blender. (Beware! If you attempt to purée before soup has cooled down, the top of the blender will blow and you will have an orange kitchen—trust me, I've been there.) The soup should have a thick and smooth consistency, but the exact thickness is a matter of taste. After blending the first two-thirds of the stock and vegetables, check the consistency of the blended soup. If it is too thin, drain off a cup (250 mL) of the stock from the unblended vegetables. If it is too thick, add the remaining cup (250 mL) of stock to the pot. Blend remaining vegetables and stock. Season to taste with nutmeg, salt, and pepper. If you prefer a rustic texture, serve as is. For extra-velvety carrot soup, pass puréed soup through a fine mesh strainer and discard any solids.

To serve, reheat to a gentle simmer. Serve in warmed bowls. If you choose to increase the richness quotient, add approximately 2 tablespoons (30 mL) of cream per serving while reheating, or drizzle a tablespoon (15 mL) overtop after the soup has been ladled into the bowls.

yield 6–8 servings level of difficulty So easy, Bugs Bunny could make it. active prep time 1 hour inactive cooking time 30 minutes advance work Can be made up to 2 days in advance. music to cook by The Neville Brothers, *Yellow Moon*. Here's hoping your soup is as smooth as Aaron Neville's voice. liquid assets A Chardonnay from Burgundy's Meursault region will help make this soup shine.

a man
&
his pan

stovetop recipes

In my day job, I serve lamb in the form of cupcakes (see page 184) and pound cake in the form of french fries (see page 212), but when I cook for myself at home, I favor healthy dishes that can be prepared quickly. The majority of these meals are made in my nonstick sauté and cast-iron pans. They rely on lots of veggies, a bit of protein, a few condiments, and as much garlic, shallots, and herbs as I can fit into the pan. Most of these dishes are done in about 10 minutes or when my ADD kicks in—whichever comes first.

the art of sautéing

SAUTÉING IS A SOPHISTICATED VERSION of pan-cooking meets wok-cooking. The sauté method is all about speed, control, versatility, and high heat, which sears the food on the outside, sealing in the moisture and flavor. As a result, your food stays moist, cooks faster, and absorbs less of the oil or butter. Once you become comfortable sautéing, you will be able to prepare fast, fresh, flava-licious meals effortlessly.

The following little primer will help you add some sizzle to your pan-cooking:

the heat

Sautéing is faster, easier, and more precise on a gas stove. Unfortunately, most of us have little choice over this crucial piece of equipment. If you are burdened with electric elements, you have two options: 1) Move. 2) Set one element to high and the other to medium-low, and toggle your pan between the two.

the pan

Sauté pans come in many sizes but one standard shape. The rounded sides are designed to allow you to turn the food with a flick of the wrist by ricocheting it off the backside of the pan (see the illustration on opposite page). Professional chefs use uncoated steel pans (also known as French steel). To avoid sticking, they grease their pans generously and keep the food moving. Nonstick pans are a home cook's best friend. They require less fat, and help prevent stickage and burning. Show these pans the respect they deserve by caressing their delicate bellies with nothing but silicone or wooden cooking utensils.

the fat

Butter, oil, and margarine all work well in the sauté pan, though I am predisposed to avoiding the latter. In order to keep butter from burning and browning, you can either clarify it (see page 248), which produces excellent results but can be a pain in the ass, or use a mixture of half butter, half oil. For general sautéing, I use an inexpensive olive oil because I like the flavor olive oil imparts. But when sautéing over very high heat, I lean toward peanut or canola oil because they have higher smoke points.

the technique

Practice your tossing technique with a cold pan and a beanbag in the privacy of your own kitchen, then graduate to a hot pan of green beans. If you tend toward exuberance, be sure to wear an apron.

☞ Pat dry meats, fish, and chicken with a paper towel or clean cloth to remove excess moisture. Prepare all other ingredients so that they are pan-ready.

☞ Preheat a dry pan on the burner over medium-high heat for about 1 minute. Add your butter and/or oil. Wait until it is bubbling or almost smoking before adding ingredients.

☞ For fast-cooking foods (e.g., shrimp, veggies, or a quick pasta sauce), start by sautéing the flavoring ingredients such as garlic, ginger, onions, or red chili flakes until the first sign of browning. This unlocks their flavors and infuses the oil, which, in turn, coats whatever is added to the pan later.

☞ For dense foods or larger cuts that take longer to cook, start cooking the main component first so that the herbs and spices are not in the pan for so long that they burn. For meats such as chicken or pork that must be fully cooked, sear the outside first on high heat and then cover the pan, reduce the heat, and finish cooking.

☞ Adjust the flame (or toggle between elements on an electric stove) so that your food doesn't burn before it cooks through.

☞ Keep it moving. Most foods will cook thoroughly and evenly over high heat if constantly turned. The exception is flat pieces of meat, which are usually only turned once.

☞ Don't be dismayed if you don't get it all right on your first attempt. Finessing the temperature and flipping like a pro is a confidence thang you will develop over time.

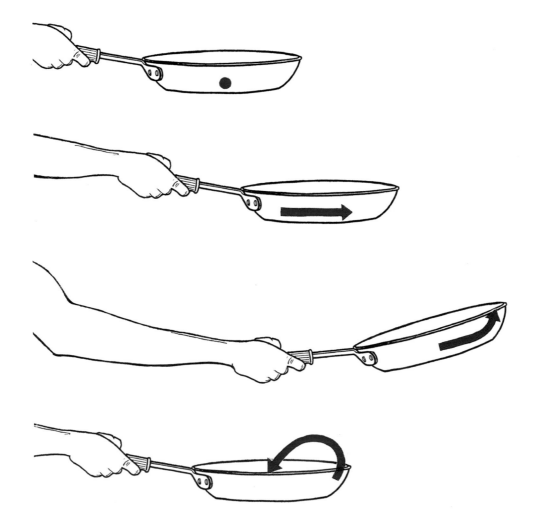

best fishes

My adolescence and college years were completely fishless. I didn't eat a single creature from the water until a meeting with David Geffen. Geffen, a mere millionaire in those days and actively running Geffen Records, was trying to sign Jane Siberry, the artist I managed. He invited me to his Malibu beach house for lunch, where his butler served up grilled salmon. For obvious reasons, I was too intimidated to refuse it. The mild flavor and pleasing texture kick-started my appreciation for fish—now bordering on an obsession.

Years later, as the Surreal Gourmet, I did a one-week *stage* at Craft, Tom Colicchio's flagship restaurant in New York City. While assisting the chef in charge of fish, I learned how to create the crispy skin and tender, moist flesh that separate restaurant-cooked fish from most home-cooked fish.

Flash forward to my fourth season of *Glutton for Punishment*. While taping a scene with Martial Noguier, the French-trained executive chef of Chicago's Sofitel hotel, I learned how to create a crispier skin and moister flesh by cooking the fillet skin side down from start to finish.

The more you learn about cooking skin-on fillets, the simpler it gets.

Four 6-ounce (175 g) skin-on fish fillets (e.g., branzini, striped bass, red snapper,
    whitefish, salmon . . .)
Salt and freshly ground black pepper
1 tablespoon (15 mL) canola, safflower, or olive oil
2 tablespoons (30 mL) butter
4 sprigs fresh thyme (optional)

Preheat oven to 350°F (180°C). Season fish with salt and pepper. Heat a heavy, ovenproof sauté pan over high heat. Add oil and set fish, skin side down, in pan. Use another pan or object to weigh down fish. Cook for approximately 3 minutes, or until skin is a crispy brown and fish is about two-thirds cooked from the bottom up. Remove weight and transfer pan to the oven. Cook until fish is no longer translucent on the top (3 to 5 minutes, depending on the thickness of the fillet).

With fish still in the pan, drain oil and return pan to the stovetop over medium-high heat. Add butter and thyme (if using). Let sizzle for 30 seconds as thyme infuses the butter. Spoon butter overtop of fish several times. Transfer, skin side up, to a plate. Top fish with the fried thyme.

yield 4 servings **level of difficulty** Pan-searing fish is easy. Doing it perfectly takes practice and finesse. **suggested accompaniment** Serve fish on sautéed spinach, a vegetable hash, my corn succotash (see page 116), or my Instant White Bean Cassoulet (see page 117). **active prep time** 5 minutes **cooking time** 15 minutes **music to cook by** Any Phish bootleg **liquid assets** Most of the types of fish I suggested are relatively mild and should pair well with a not-too-tannic wine of any persuasion.

licorice shrimp

Several years ago, I was approached to write a monthly column for *Highways*, a magazine for RV enthusiasts. Other than for the obvious connection of my Toastermobile, I wasn't sure at first if I could connect with the RV audience. Then I realized that the challenges of cooking in the ill-equipped, cramped quarters of an RV kitchen are not much different than the challenges many people face at home.

Five years later, I am still writing the column. The recipes I create are designed to be made in one or two pans with minimum prep space and time. (Clearly these people have things to do and places to go.) At first, the combination of shrimp and licorice flavors may seem like an unlikely coupling, but just like me and the RV community, it's a natural pairing.

½ medium-size fennel bulb (ideally with fronds intact)
2 tablespoons (30 mL) butter
10 ounces (300 g) 21/25 count raw shrimp (or any medium size), peeled and deveined
2 ounces (60 mL) Pernod or any other licorice-based flavored liqueur (pastis or sambuca)
¼ teaspoon (1 mL) chili pepper flakes
1 cup (250 mL) canned crushed tomatoes (ideally San Marzano)
¼ cup (60 mL) half-and-half cream
¼ cup (60 mL) chicken stock
1 tablespoon (15 mL) freshly squeezed lemon juice
Salt and freshly ground black pepper
2 slices rustic bread, toasted

Before flambéing, see Fire Regulations (page 249).

Core and finely dice fennel bulb. Reserve fronds.

In a sauté pan over high heat, add butter and fennel. Sauté for 2 minutes. Add shrimp and sauté for 1 to 2 minutes, turning once, or until shrimp begin to lose their translucency.

Add Pernod, let sit for 5 seconds, and then light a match to it. The flame should burn out after approximately 10 seconds. (If flame continues to burn, put it out by placing a lid on the pan.) Allow liquids to reduce for 20 seconds. Add chili flakes and tomatoes, and simmer for 2 minutes. Add cream, stock, and lemon juice. Reduce for 1 to 2 minutes, or until sauce is thick and rich. Season to taste with salt and pepper.

Serve in shallow bowls alongside toast (to sop up the sauce), and garnish with fennel fronds.

yield 2 servings **level of difficulty** If you can build and light a fire, you can make this dish. **active prep time** 5 minutes **cooking time** 10 minutes **shortcuts** Eat it straight from the pan. **music to cook by** Massive Attack, *Mezzanine*. Richly layered textures and sounds. **liquid assets** Chianti Classico has the earth and acidity to play with the diverse elements of the dish.

five-minute aglio olio

Preparing an entrée from scratch in under 10 minutes is a push for most home cooks. But for a line cook in a restaurant, that amount of time is considered a luxury. In *Glutton for Punishment*, one of the most difficult challenges I took on was stepping into the shoes of these foot soldiers of the kitchen. My first such challenge was attempting to be lead egg cook at Harrah's casino in Atlantic City, in a café that serves up a million eggs a year. It was such an adrenaline-filled episode that two seasons later, I trained to be the lead pasta cook at Chicago's Mia Francesca, which serves up 600 orders of pasta on a busy night. In both cases, I flamed out at the end, but in the process, I developed a new skill set—and a whole new level of respect for the unsung heroes of the line.

This recipe is my interpretation of the classic Italian dish. Any self-respecting line cook would knock it out, start to finish, in about 90 seconds. I'm confident that in the peaceful serenity of your own kitchen you can cinch it in five minutes.

1 tablespoon (15 mL) salt
2 servings fresh angel-hair pasta or spaghetti (or dried, if you have an extra
    2 or 3 minutes to spare)
3 tablespoons (45 mL) olive oil
4 cloves garlic, minced
½–1 teaspoon (2–5 mL) chili pepper flakes (depending on your heat tolerance)
Zest of 1 lemon
½ cup (125 mL) finely chopped fresh Italian parsley (stems discarded)
½ teaspoon (2 mL) freshly ground black pepper
¼ cup (60 mL) (about 1 ounce/30 g) freshly grated Parmigiano Reggiano

Bring a large pot of water to a boil, and set a sauté pan over medium-high heat. Add salt to the water, then add pasta. Cook according to directions.

Add oil to the pan, let it heat up for a few seconds, then add garlic and chili flakes. Sauté for approximately 30 seconds, or until garlic just begins to turn golden. Remove from heat until pasta is cooked. Reserve ¼ cup (60 mL) of pasta water. Drain pasta. Return pan to heat, and add pasta and reserved pasta water. Toss. Add zest, parsley, and black pepper. Toss thoroughly, and top with Parmigiano Reggiano. Serve immediately.

yield Serves 2 hungry, impatient diners le secret Tossing the pasta in the pan at the end and adding pasta water is a classic Italian trick for coating pasta with flavor instead of just topping it. level of difficulty If you can heat a can of SpaghettiOs, you can make this dish. one step beyond To transform your aglio olio into an instant puttanesca, add a few anchovies along with the garlic and chili flakes. After the garlic has just begun to turn golden, add 1 cup (250 mL) of crushed canned tomatoes (ideally San Marzano), 1 tablespoon (15 mL) of drained capers, a palmful of pitted olives, and ½ teaspoon (2 mL) of dried oregano, basil, or thyme. Let simmer for a couple of minutes before adding the pasta and pasta water. active prep time 2–5 minutes cooking time 2–5 minutes shortcuts It's hard to shave time off a 5-minute recipe! music to cook by If you've got any classic Italian opera, now's the time to play it. liquid assets Any hearty Italian red will do the trick.

lucky duck

Duck has the texture of a fine cut of steak, but a flavor that is deeper and far more distinctive. That's why it's a perennial favorite of French chefs. Cooking a whole duck can be an unwieldy experience because of the thick layer of fat that insulates it. Fortunately for those of us whose kitchens don't come equipped with six-burner stoves and an army of sous chefs, duck breasts deliver all the flavor without the fuss. Don't be put off by duck's unusual look. The fat-to-meat proportions reverse in the cooking process as the fat melts away and the meat expands. (Pictured with Unsuffering Succotash, page 116.)

Two 6- to 8-ounce (175–250 g) boneless duck breasts
½ teaspoon (2 mL) salt
1½ teaspoons (7.5 mL) coarsely ground pepper, divided
2 shallots, finely diced
2 tablespoons (30 mL) balsamic vinegar
¼ cup (60 mL) black currant jam (ideally unsweetened), black cherry jam, or similar preserve
2 tablespoons (30 mL) crème de cassis

Preheat oven to 350°F (180°C) and set out a cookie sheet lined with aluminum foil.

Use a paper towel to pat dry duck. Using a sharp knife, score four ¼-inch-deep (6 mm) cuts across the duck skin at a 45-degree angle (see diagram page 255.) Sprinkle ¼ teaspoon (1 mL) of salt and ¼ teaspoon (1 mL) of pepper over the meat side of each duck breast.

Heat a medium-size heavy pan over high heat. When pan is hot, add duck breasts to the dry pan, skin side down, and cook for approximately 5 minutes, or until skin is brown and crispy. Flip and cook for 2 more minutes.

Remove pan from heat, reserve the drippings in pan, and transfer duck breasts, skin side up, to cookie sheet. Bake on the top rack of the oven for 5 minutes (7 minutes if you are using the thicker Muscovy breasts).

While duck is roasting, carefully discard all but 2 tablespoons (30 mL) of duck drippings from the pan. Return pan to medium heat and add shallots. Stir occasionally for 3 minutes, or until shallots begin to turn golden. Remove from heat, add vinegar to the pan and stir with a wooden spoon to loosen up the browned bits left by the duck. Add jam, cassis, and remaining pepper. Return to heat and stir occasionally for 3 minutes. Reserve.

Remove duck from the oven, cover with aluminum foil, and let rest for 5 minutes. Slice each breast at a 45-degree angle into ¼-inch-thick (6 mm) strips (properly cooked duck should resemble medium-rare steak). Arrange in a fanlike pattern on a warmed plate and spoon cassis compote overtop or alongside. Serve immediately.

yield 2 servings uncommon goods Duck breasts are available in fancy groceries and at specialty butchers. They are often kept in the frozen food section. They may come as one butterflied breast. If so,

(continued . . .)

(. . . continued)

slice down the middle to separate them. My favorite ducks are Muscovy ducks, but any duck will fit the bill. Crème de cassis is a syrupy liqueur made from black currants. Cointreau or Grand Marnier may be substituted, and will add an orangey twist to your sauce. le secret The only trick is learning to ignore the instinct to overcook the duck. level of difficulty Once you are comfortable with cooking poultry medium-rare, it's as easy as cooking a chicken breast. active prep time 10 minutes cooking time 20 minutes advance work Duck and sauce can be prepared an hour in advance. In this case, the duck should be slightly undercooked and left uncut. Reheat in a 425°F (220°C) oven for 3 to 4 minutes just before slicing and serving. Sauce should be rewarmed just before serving. music to cook by Serge Gainsbourg, *Comic Strip*. The once-banned, now-revered (but still dead) French provocateur at his pop peak. liquid assets Côte de Nuits (a red burgundy), or a Santa Barbara or Oregon Pinot Noir. Any of these wines should provide a supple, jammy quality that will waddle well with the sauce.

unsuffering succotash

I make this recipe several times a week in the summertime, when farmers' markets offer up insanely sweet corn at irresistibly low prices. Its contents vary slightly, depending on whatever additional seasonal veggies are in my fridge. But the result is always a bright, happy-go-lucky side dish that works well with just about any meat, fish, or poultry you toss on the grill or in a pan.

1 tablespoon (15 mL) olive oil
1 tablespoon (15 mL) butter
2 slices smoky bacon, sliced crosswise in ¼-inch-thick (6 mm) strips
½ yam, peeled and diced in ¼-inch (6 mm) cubes
2 cloves garlic, minced
1 shallot, diced
½ cup (125 mL) fresh or frozen lima or fava beans
½ red bell pepper, finely diced
4 ears corn, kernels cut from cob, or 2 cups (500 mL) frozen corn, thawed
2 tablespoons (30 mL) finely chopped fresh thyme or tarragon (stems discarded)
¼ teaspoon (1 mL) ground dried chipotle or a pinch of cayenne pepper
Salt and freshly ground black pepper
2 tablespoons (30 mL) freshly squeezed lime juice

In a large sauté pan over medium heat, add oil, butter, bacon, and yam. Cover and cook for about 10 minutes, or until bacon renders and yam softens.

Remove cover, add garlic and shallot, and cook for 10 more minutes, or until bacon begins to crisp and veggies begin to brown.

Add beans, bell pepper, and corn. Cook for 10 more minutes, stirring occasionally. Finish with thyme, chipotle, salt and pepper to taste, and lime juice.

yield Serves 4 as a side dish **active prep time** 10 minutes **cooking time** 30 minutes **advance work** Can be made earlier in the day and reheated just before serving.

instant white bean cassoulet

The original version of this classic French dish requires such a long time to prepare, it's no wonder that the French government felt obliged to initiate a 35-hour work week. In order to help you stew your beans *and* still have time to eat them, I've created a simple version that you can knock out in 15 minutes flat.

2 tablespoons (30 mL) olive oil
4 ounces (125 g) pancetta or bacon, sliced crosswise in ¼-inch (6 mm) strips
4 cloves garlic, minced
2 shallots, diced
One 14-ounce (398 mL) can white beans (ideally large beans), drained and rinsed
2 cups (500 mL) mustard greens, dandelion greens, Swiss chard, or spinach
¼ cup (60 mL) chicken stock
Salt and freshly ground black pepper

Heat a sauté pan over medium-high heat. Add oil and pancetta. Cook for 3 minutes, then add garlic and shallots. Cook for 2 minutes, or until garlic starts to brown, then add beans. Cook for 3 more minutes, stirring occasionally, then add greens and stock. Cover and cook for a few more minutes until greens wilt. Season with salt and pepper.

yield Serves 4 as a side dish **active prep time** 5 minutes **cooking time** 15 minutes **advance work** Can be made earlier in the day and reheated just before serving.

bacon 'n' brussels sprouts

This winter-licious side may sound like old-school British pub food, but its addictive, earthy flavor will make you reconsider your aversion to Brussels sprouts.

1 tablespoon (15 mL) olive oil
3 slices bacon, sliced in ¼-inch (6 mm) strips
½ yellow onion, diced
1 pound (500 g) Brussels sprouts, chiffonaded (sliced finely, not necessarily accurately)
Salt and freshly ground black pepper
1 tablespoon (15 mL) freshly squeezed lemon juice

In your largest sauté pan, over medium-high heat, add oil and bacon. Stir occasionally for 3 minutes, or until bacon begins to render. Add onion and stir occasionally for another 3 minutes, or until onion begins to soften. Add sprouts and ½ cup (125 mL) water. Cover tightly. Let steam for 6 to 8 minutes, or until water has evaporated and sprouts have softened. Remove lid and cook for another 5 to 10 minutes, stirring occasionally, until the whole lot has wilted and started to brown. Finish with salt, pepper, and lemon juice.

yield Serves 4 as a side dish **active prep time** 10 minutes **cooking time** 25 minutes **advance work** Can be made earlier in the day and reheated just before serving.

liar, liar, pants on fire

Within months of the release of my first book in 1993, I was invited by the Art Gallery of New South Wales in Sydney, Australia, to participate in a series of events in conjunction with a major exhibition of surrealist art. It was an offer I couldn't refuse. I'd been to Australia twice before and loved the carefree attitude, surf culture, beer, and especially their affinity for taking the piss out of each other. "Cutting down the tallest poppy," they call it. In order to justify the long haul, I encouraged my publisher to try to pull together a couple of additional media events. I was anticipating a pleasant vacation of sunning and surfing, interspersed with the occasional interview. What I did not expect was an experience that was so embarrassing I didn't tell a soul for 10 years.

Life is sweet, I thought as I settled into my cramped quarters on a Qantas 747. Three movies, a pulp fiction novel, six compact discs, and four screwdrivers later, I was in Sydney, staring in disbelief at a jam-packed itinerary. It detailed seven days of press, including eight TV appearances, three newspaper interviews, four book signings, and a department store demonstration. So much for surfing. Scheduled between the morning show appearances and cooking programs were two variety show bookings: *Live and Sweaty*, an irreverent improv show, and *Tonight Live with Steve Vizard*, a late-night talk show. Even though I was a neophyte on the book-flogging circuit, I was already savvy enough to recognize that these were highly coveted appearances. Each one provided a rare opportunity to reach the elusive and highly sought-after "young, hip audience."

My appearance on *Tonight Live* was clearly the crown jewel in my promo tour. In fact, it was important enough that a few days before my arrival, I was pre-interviewed over the phone by a segment producer. Pre-interviews involve a one-sided game of 20 questions during which the interrogator attempts to isolate the stories and shticks from the interviewee's repertoire that best fit the format of the show. The interrogator also distills the information into questions for the hosts to ask so they can appear well prepared for the segment—even though chances are they have never read the book, listened to the CD, or seen the movie.

A day later, the segment producer called to say he wanted me to reprise a bit of culinary theatrics that went over well on an appearance on the fledgling US Food Network. I would prepare steak au poivre, and Steve and I would dress in firefighters' regalia to protect us from the flames that leap from the pan when the cognac is ignited. It was just enough of a performance art gag to elevate the bit into the kind of comedy that the producer hoped would play well with his late-night audience.

I'm excited as I arrive at the studio for the afternoon taping. I have my own dressing room and all the star-treatment accoutrements I have often heard about, but never experienced. Before I know it, I am being led downstairs to the studio entrance. Through a curtain, the audience-warm-up comedian is plying his trade. "Who's here from out of town? . . . We've got a great show for you tonight, including actress Angel Reed; Bob Blumer, a wacky chef from California . . . and a big surprise . . . I know you are going to have a great time." I tune him out and rehearse a few jokes that I hope to casually drop into my conversation with Steve. Since I had only made a few TV appearances stateside before my Australian trip, and never one on late-night TV, this is my attempt to prepare myself for the comedy element of the show.

After a Lettermanesque opening monologue, a pretty, slender actress from Melbourne sashays onstage to swap witticisms and pitch her new film. Then Steve does a live satellite interview with a hometown sportscaster covering a big footie match in Italy. As the interview winds down, the floor producer signals that I am on in one minute. My stomach churns.

"Next up we have a man who is a cook. But not just any cook, he's a surreal cook. Please welcome—Bob Blumer," says Steve. The band kicks into two bars of a jazz funk sting as I walk out to a makeshift cooking setup. At the lip of the stage, there is a small card table holding my ingredients, a Bunsen burner, a sauté pan, and a propped-up copy of my book.

"Now let's get straight into this," Steve tells the audience. "Bob's going to cook for us, so can we have a couple of volunteers down here to help him out?"

Volunteers? I search my mind for any recollection of a discussion about volunteers. "Whatever," I think to myself as I prepare to go with the flow.

"What are you going to make for us, Bob?"

"Steak au poivre."

"For those of you at home, that's pepper steak. Now let's welcome . . . what's your name?" Steve asks a woman with a large mane of frizzy blonde hair who has crawled over several audience members to get to the aisle and down to the stage.

"I'm Joanne," she says breathlessly.

"Welcome, Joanne." (Polite audience applause.)

Scanning the crowd, Steve points at a demure man at the end of the third row. "What's your name?"

"Uh . . . I'm Eddie."

"Come on down, Eddie."

The guy stands up hesitantly and plods to the stage.

"Now, Bob, how would you describe your style of cooking?" Steve asks, refocusing my attention.

"I call it recipes for the cooking impaired. Everything I make is thrown together very quickly using lots of fresh ingredients. If you shop well, the ingredients do all the hard work for you," I say, repeating the culinary mantra of my early days.

As I reach for the delicate six-ounce pieces of filet mignon, Steve quips: "You call that a steak, Bob?"

"That's a Californian portion," I respond with one of my prepared retorts.

"Now while you're taking us through the recipe, let's get these guys to jump in and lend you a hand."

Joanne acts on cue and grabs the salt and pepper grinder to season the meat. This is great because it allows me to stay in the game with Steve. Eddie, on the other hand, clearly doesn't have a culinary bone in his body, and has randomly grabbed the Dijon mustard, which he is trying to add to the pan.

"Not yet, Eddie," I say.

Meanwhile, Steve drives the segment forward. "According to your book, you don't take more than 30 minutes to make any of your recipes . . ."

"That's right. I always put on a CD to police myself when I'm making dinner. It's a bit of a twist on musical chairs—if the disc ends before I'm finished cooking, I know it's time to get out of the kitchen." I drop the steaks into the sizzling butter. "I know these steaks may look small to you, but the portion sizes here in Australia make Fred Flintstone look like he's on a diet." That crack wins a smattering of chuckles from the studio audience and I begin to feel a little more self-assured.

Eddie, who is proving himself to be a complete idiot, grabs the carton of cream and attempts to pour it in the pan.

"Not yet, Eddie," I say again, more firmly this time.

I pause to look around and revel in the moment. Hey, this late-night gig isn't so tough after all. With my newfound sense of confidence, I launch into our preplanned gag. "Now, Steve, they tell me you're a big man on campus here in Australia, which makes me a little nervous to be willfully setting a fire right under your nose. To protect you, I've brought along some special gear." The audience guffaws as I reveal the regulation firefighter's outfit borrowed from the Sydney Fire Department. Steve puts on the helmet, and I slip into the jacket.

"You guys are on your own," Steve warns Joanne and Eddie as he pulls the plastic visor down over his face. "Anyone can do this, can't they, Bob?" he asks.

"Sure," I enthuse. "Flambéing is easy, impressive, and not really as dangerous as it looks."

"What are the green peppercorns for?" Eddie-the-idiot blurts out as he reaches across the table for the jar.

"We'll get to them in a minute," I respond, moving the jar out of range. The guy is really beginning to get on my nerves.

By this time, the steaks are cooked. I grab the cognac bottle and pour a generous splash into the pan. On TV I always use a little extra so that the flames are more dramatic. It sizzles appetizingly. The audience oohs and ahhs. I touch a match to the liquid. Just as it ignites, Eddie-the-idiot lunges forward to grab the peppercorns from the front of the table. As his arm extends over the now-blazing pan, the flame catches the left sleeve of his sports jacket, and to my horror his entire arm erupts into a ball of fire.

The audience draws a collective sharp breath, and Eddie-the-idiot panics. He stumbles forward, crashing into the wobbly table, sending the ingredients flying like shrapnel in all directions. Seconds later, my book lies in a puddle of cognac and cream, the Dijon mustard is splattered across the studio floor like a Jackson Pollock painting, and there is broken glass everywhere. It's hard to image so much carnage in so little time.

The steaks are still on fire—as is Eddie. All eyes are glued on him as he runs in circles around the studio, flailing his left arm wildly in the air. This action fans the flames and exacerbates the fire. The stagehands rush the stage, and audience members begin streaming for the exit. Finally someone emerges with a bucket of water and Eddie plunges his arm in it. The water hisses, a white puff of steam rises from the bucket, and the damage is finally contained.

Anyone anywhere on the Australian continent who tunes in later that night sees me frozen in a state of shock, looking like the proverbial deer caught in the headlights. As I stand there with my heart palpitating, my mind is racing with thoughts of inevitable lawsuits, my short-lived cooking career, my unfinished steak au poivre, and, of course, poor—albeit stupid—Eddie. I look up at the remaining audience members. Only moments ago they were eating out of the palm of my hand, but now they are glaring at me as if I were the Antichrist.

Steve, the consummate professional, calmly announces that we're going to take a commercial break. The band comes to the rescue by kicking into a song, and we go off the air to regroup.

Stagehands mop up the mess as I stand there, dazed. I am not even really aware of the time that passes. Steve takes me by the arm, leads me up to the guest sofa, and sits me down beside the petite actress. She seems more concerned with her hair then my pathetic predicament. He whispers something in her ear, then leans over to me and gives me an assuring pat on the shoulder as if to say, "Don't worry, mate, shit happens."

The floor producer counts down from five and points to Steve. "Welcome back," he says, looking into the camera. He assures the television audience that Eddie is OK, and then thanks the actress and myself for being on the show. I make a stab at regaining my self-respect by attempting a weak joke: "If you can't stand the heat, get out of the kitchen." As the band launches into the show's closing theme song, we all smile and wave good-bye. Then, mercifully, this dark episode in my life is over.

I am still traumatized as I slink out the rear exit of the studio with my jacket pulled over my head like a white-collar criminal leaving a courtroom. I get back to my hotel room, close the door, and collapse on the bed, staring at the ceiling in disbelief. How could a simple cooking segment have gone so awry? Why didn't they screen the volunteers? How will I ever live this down? I replay the scenario over and over in my head. My self-flagellating is interrupted by a knock on the door. I contemplate hiding, but snap myself out of my funk long enough to get up and peer through the peephole. In the bright light of the hallway, a bellhop stands with what appears to be a bottle of Scotch. At this point, I really need a drink, so I open the door just wide enough to grab the bottle. As I slam the door shut, I notice that there is a small note attached. It reads:

Dear Mr. Blumer,

Thanks for being such a good sport.

Best wishes,
Steve Vizard

In a flash, the entire ruse becomes painfully obvious. The warm-up comedian's promise of a big surprise, the oddly situated demo table, the unexpected "volunteers," the reassuring whisper to the actress. My eyes widen and my heart beats even faster. THOSE FUCKERS. The whole thing was a setup. Eddie-the-idiot was obviously a stunt man—and *I* was the idiot.

At that point, you would think that the humiliation would be over. But that would be wishful thinking. Anyone who might have missed the original broadcast was treated to an encore performance when the segment was featured on *Tonight Live*'s popular year-end best-of show.

Seventeen years later, with plenty of hindsight, I think it's about the funniest thing that has ever happened to me in my unlikely career as a globe-trotting gourmand. In retrospect, it was also one of the best things. It taught me to loosen up and not to take myself, or what I do, too seriously—it's pepper steak, after all, not neurosurgery. And given my affinity for the Aussies' unique brand of humor, how could I protest being used to prove that it is alive and thriving?

classic steak au poivre

Try and keep the flames in the pan!

1 teaspoon (5 mL) salt
4 teaspoons (20 mL) coarsely ground black pepper
Four 6-ounce (175 g), ¾-inch-thick (2 cm) tenderloin steaks
1 tablespoon (15 mL) butter
2 ounces (60 mL) cognac or brandy
1 tablespoon (15 mL) Dijon mustard
⅔ cup (160 mL) half-and-half cream
3 tablespoons (45 mL) brined green peppercorns (drained)

Before flambéing, see Fire Regulations (page 249).

Rub salt and ground black pepper over both sides of the steaks.

Heat a dry sauté pan over high heat. When pan becomes very hot, add butter, let melt, then add steaks. Turn steaks only once, and cook to desired degree of wellness (approximately 3 minutes per side for medium-rare, depending on exact thickness). To avoid overcooking, make an incision in the middle of the steak to check the color.

Add cognac to pan, let sit for 5 seconds, then light a match to it. The flame should burn out after approximately 10 seconds. (If flame continues to burn, put it out by placing a lid on the pan.)

Remove steak from pan (leaving drippings in the pan). Cover steak with aluminum foil.

Reduce heat to low and slowly stir Dijon and cream into the drippings. Add peppercorns. Stir and simmer for a couple of minutes until sauce gains some thickness.

Pour sauce over steak, and serve.

yield 4 servings **le secret** Don't invite any strangers to be your sous chef! **level of difficulty** No more difficult than pan-cooking a burger. **active prep time** 5 minutes **cooking time** 15 minutes **music to cook by** Midnight Oil, *Diesel and Dust*. Contains the politically charged hit "Beds Are Burning." **liquid assets** If you are sitting on any Penfolds Grange, now's the time to open it. Otherwise, an earthy Shiraz will do nicely.

on "Q"

BBQ recipes

My dad was an avid backyard griller and the original Patio Daddy-O. He didn't approve of briquettes and only used real hardwood charcoal, which he lit with rolled-up newspaper to avoid contaminating the coals with the smell of lighter fluid.

Like father, like son. My first grill was a hibachi that I bought at my local hardware store. Eventually I graduated to a Weber kettle. In my first book, I proudly pontificated: "The best grill flavor comes from real hardwood charcoal."

Years later, in a one-on-one professional training seminar from Weber grills with Elizabeth Karmel (who would later become my grilling guru, and with whom I coauthored *Pizza on the Grill*), I learned that in many cases gas grills can deliver flavors that are indistinguishable from charcoal. This is especially relevant for foods that don't spend much time on the grill. Their flavor comes from the inherent proteins and natural sugars that caramelize over any source of direct high heat—creating the distinctive brown crust that makes grilled food so appealing.

Gas grills are also infinitely more inviting. Since adding one alongside my Weber kettle, I gravitate to grilling far more frequently, sadly ignoring the kettle (and the charcoal) that I championed for so many years. I still fire up "old faithful" occasionally for thick slabs of meat, but the rest of the time it's turn, ignite, and grill.

lettuce leaves salmon, and is grilled

It's a creative cooking technique . . . It's a clever presentation trick . . . It's foolproof fish on the grill . . . It's "Supersalmon" in a lettuce cape! The roots of this dish originated in France, where *chefs de cuisine* still wrap pigeons in radicchio leaves and roast them. In North America, such a dish would qualify as a bona fide buzzkill at any dinner party. So I modified the ingredients to fit the popular palate and to take the guesswork out of grilling fish.

8 large romaine lettuce leaves
¼ cup (60 mL) olive oil
Four 6-ounce (175 g) salmon fillets or steaks
Salt and freshly ground black pepper
2 lemons—1 halved for juicing, 1 sliced
4 teaspoons (20 mL) capers
8 sprigs fresh dill

Four 3-foot (90 cm) pieces of twine (or another
   nonflammable natural fiber)

Soak twine in warm water for 5 minutes.

Preheat grill to high direct heat (see page 247).

Rinse romaine leaves in cold water. Shake, but do not dry. Rub oil generously over the inside (concave) side of each of the lettuce leaves.

Set out your 4 largest leaves, concave side up. Place a salmon fillet in center of each leaf. Season each fillet with salt and pepper and drizzle with lemon juice. Spoon 1 teaspoon (5 mL) of capers overtop each fillet, then top each with a lemon slice and 2 sprigs of dill.

Place a second leaf over the salmon, fold ends of bottom leaf up to keep juices trapped, and wrap twine around leaves to seal (see diagram page 255). Tie the twine in a knot.

Grill the salmon for approximately 3 to 4 minutes per side. Cooking time will vary according to its thickness. Keep track of which side has the capers and dill (usually the side with the knot), and set that side up. Serve with a pair of scissors.

yield 4 servings uncommon goods Twine; scissors le secret Do not overcook the salmon. To test, make an incision in the middle. Tastes vary, but most people like their salmon light pink with just a faint hint of red in the very center. adventure club Go catch the salmon yourself. level of diffi-culty As simple as wrapping a gift and flipping a burger. active prep time 20 minutes grilling time 10 minutes advance work The neatly wrapped bundles of salmon can be made hours in advance and stacked upon themselves in the refrigerator, making this dish a winner for parties of any size. oven version Salmon bundles can be broiled for approximately 5 minutes per side. music to cook by Leonard Cohen, *I'm Your Man.* Leonard *is* the man. liquid assets Pinot noirs from Sonoma's Russian River region rarely fail to deliver luscious fruit and supple mouthfeel.

beer can chicken

As soon as I heard about Beer Can Chicken, I knew it was right up my alley. Why, even Salvador Dalí couldn't have come up with a more playfully shocking art piece than a four-pound roaster pirouetting atop a can of Bud.

But the visuals are just the beginning. You will never experience chicken that delivers so much pleasure for so little effort. Who knew that a can of beer could be so functional? It's an upright roaster, allowing the skin to self-baste in its own fat to crispy perfection, and the beer steams and infuses the bird, making the meat fall-off-the-bone moist. You get a perfect bird each time, every time.

When I made this on the *Today Show*, Katie Couric took one look and said, "Dr. Freud, call your office." Rest assured the chicken is having as much fun as you are.

One 4-pound (1.8–2.2 kg) whole chicken
2 tablespoons (30 mL) vegetable oil
3 tablespoons (45 mL) of your favorite dry spice rub
2 tablespoons (30 mL) sea salt or kosher salt
1 baby potato, head of garlic, or shallot (for plugging chicken)
1 can of beer

Preset grill on high for indirect cooking (see page 247).

Remove neck and giblets. Rinse chicken inside and out; pat dry with paper towels. Rub chicken lightly with oil, then rub inside and out with dry rub and salt. Reserve.

Open beer can and sip or drain off one-third of the beer. Place beer can on a solid surface, grab a chicken leg in each hand, and plunk the bird cavity over the beer can. Adjust if necessary so that the bird is sitting upright. Stuff potato, garlic, or shallot in the small top cavity of the bird and pull loose skin overtop to seal. Transfer the bird-on-a-can to your grill and place in the center of the grate, balancing the bird on its 2 legs and the can like a tripod. Close lid.

Cook chicken for approximately 1¼ hours, or until the internal temperature registers 165°F (74°C) in the breast area and 180°F (82°C) in the thigh, or until the thigh juice runs clear when stabbed with a sharp knife. Remove from grill (being careful not to spill contents of beer can, as they will be very hot) and let rest for 10 minutes before extracting beer can and carving.

yield 4 servings **le secret** Make sure that the bird is well balanced before closing lid. Otherwise the chicken may tip, spilling the beer. **level of difficulty** Way easier than making rotisserie chicken. **active prep time** 10 minutes **inactive grilling time** 1¼ hours **advance work** Can be fully cooked before guests arrive. Keep the chicken on the beer can, wrapped in foil, until ready to slice. But why deprive your guests of the vision? **oven version** Can be set on a sheet pan and baked in a 375°F (190°C) oven for approximately 1¼ hours. **music to cook by** Merle Haggard, *Drinkin'* From a man who knows. **liquid assets** The other 5 beers.

gilded trout

I love bacon so much that I am currently working on a bacon-wrapped bacon recipe, and a webcast called *Saving Your Bacon*. (Stay tuned!) I'll put it on just about anything (as evidenced by my Maple Bacon–Crunch Ice Cream; see page 160). Even cardboard tastes good when swathed in bacon. So it should come as no surprise that if you take a trout (available in grocery stores and babbling brooks everywhere), stuff it with fresh sage, and wrap it like a mummy with a half dozen strips of bacon, it will taste golden.

Four 10-ounce (300 g) trout (heads and tails on), gutted
2 tablespoons (30 mL) olive oil
Salt and freshly ground black pepper
2 lemons, sliced
4 large sprigs fresh sage
1½ pounds (750 g) sliced bacon

toothpicks

Preheat grill to medium-high direct heat (see page 247).

Rinse and pat dry fish inside and out. Drizzle the cavity of each trout with olive oil. Season with salt and pepper. Stuff each cavity with 4 lemon slices and 1 sprig of sage.

Wrap each trout with bacon like a mummy, using toothpicks to hold bacon in place. Each trout will require about 6 strips of bacon.

Grill for approximately 5 minutes per side, or until bacon is crispy and trout is cooked throughout (make a tiny incision to check that the flesh is no longer translucent).

yield 4 servings **le secret** Moderate the heat so that the bacon doesn't burn before the fish is cooked. **level of difficulty** As easy as wrapping a gift, then putting it on the BBQ. **active prep time** 10 minutes **grilling time** 10 minutes **advance work** Trout can be wrapped in bacon earlier in the day and refrigerated. **pan version** Trout can be pan-seared in a covered dry pan over medium-high heat for approximately 5 minutes per side. **music to cook by** Goldfrapp, *Supernature*. A glam-tastic channeling of T. Rex. **liquid assets** A gamey Chateauneuf-du-Pape will reel in the smoky flavors of the grill and the bacon.

maple-icious salmon

This remarkably easy four-ingredient recipe creates a candied salmon fillet that melts in your mouth. And the black-pepper crust provides the perfect counterpoint. The exact proportions of the closely guarded recipe were divulged, after several hours on the torture rack, by Andrew Zimbel, owner of the Toronto catering company The Amazing Food Service. It's so maple-icious that even people who don't like fish become devoted converts after just one bite.

¾ cup (185 mL) maple syrup
¼ cup (60 mL) soy sauce
Four 6-ounce (175 g) salmon fillets, skin removed
¼ cup (60 mL) coarsely ground black pepper (Grind it yourself, or purchase "cracked" pepper at your grocery store.)

In a small, deep bowl, or a resealable plastic bag, mix maple syrup and soy sauce. Add fillets so that marinade completely covers fish. Marinate in the refrigerator for as long as possible (a minimum of 4 hours, but ideally 24 to 48). Turn salmon (or bag) every few hours.

Preheat grill to medium-high direct heat (see page 247).

Place pepper on a plate. Remove salmon from marinade and pat top side into pepper to coat.

Grill for approximately 3 minutes per side, starting with pepper side down, or until salmon is just on the verge of turning opaque.

yield 4 servings **le secret** The longer the salmon marinates, the deeper the flavor. Avoid over-cooking the fillets. Salmon is best when the color has turned to a pale pink but the fish is still moist throughout. **level of difficulty** The salmon worked hard to swim upstream; you get the easy job. **active prep time** 10 minutes **inactive prep time** 4–48 hours **grilling time** 10 minutes **advance work** Salmon can be placed in its marinade up to 48 hours in advance. It should only be peppered and grilled just before serving. **multiplicity** When multiplying the recipe for larger groups, it is not necessary to increase the marinade proportionately. Just mix enough marinade (in the same proportions: 3 parts maple syrup to 1 part soy sauce) to cover all the fillets. **oven version** Salmon can also be baked on an oiled cookie sheet in a preheated 500°F (260°C) oven for approximately 6 to 8 minutes. There's no need to flip it during cooking. **music to cook by** The Cocteau Twins, *Heaven or Las Vegas*. Ethereal music to marinate your mind. **liquid assets** The sweetness of the maple combined with the umami of the soy sauce and the bite of the black pepper make this a confounding dish to pair with wine. Play it safe with an India Pale Ale.

love me tenderloin

This chili-rubbed filet mignon puts up a hot and fiery front that will tease your tongue. But deep inside lies a sweet and tender soul that will melt in your mouth. (Pictured with Smashed Potatoes, page 136.)

2 tablespoons (30 mL) New Mexico chili powder or any other pure chili powder
1 tablespoon (15 mL) ground dried chipotle (if available) or 1 additional tablespoon (15 mL) New Mexico chili powder
2 tablespoons (30 mL) granulated sugar
1 tablespoon (15 mL) freshly ground black pepper
One 2-pound (1 kg) whole fillet beef tenderloin (cut from the large end, which should be approximately 4 inches/10 cm in diameter)
1 tablespoon (15 mL) sea salt or kosher salt

In a medium bowl, combine chili powders, sugar, and black pepper.

Generously coat and pat down tenderloin with rub mixture. Wrap in waxed paper or plastic wrap and let sit at room temperature for 30 minutes.

Set grill to medium-high indirect heat (see page 247).

Just before grilling, pat down tenderloin with salt. Cook meat for 3 minutes directly over the heat source. Then rotate a quarter turn and cook for another 3 minutes. Follow the same procedure for the remaining 2 sides. When all sides have been seared (and probably blackened), transfer meat to the side of the grill that is not over any direct heat source. Cover grill and cook for 15 to 20 more minutes, turning once, or until fillet has reached your desired degree of doneness.

Place meat on a plate and cover with aluminum foil. Let rest for 10 minutes before slicing.

yield 4 servings uncommon goods Smaller precut pieces of tenderloin are available in the meat section of most grocery stores, but the large cut required for this recipe will need to be specially prepared by a butcher. (Ask him or her to bind it with twine.) Don't be shocked when you see the price per pound (about $15 to $20; per kilogram it'll be $33 to $44). I promise you, it will be well worth it. level of difficulty The only difficult part is paying for the steak. active prep time 10 minutes inactive prep time 30 minutes grilling time 40 minutes advance work The meat can be left in its dry rub for up to a day in the refrigerator. note about pan version Dry chilies, hot pans, and kitchen smoke alarms do not mix well. (Again, I speak from experience.) music to cook by Rent a karaoke machine and do your own rendition of "Love Me Tender" while you cook. liquid assets This luscious chili-rubbed steak begs for a big, spicy California Zinfandel to temper its fire.

smashed potatoes

I am an unrepentant potato slut. As soon as I see a well-prepared spud, my willpower disappears and, despite my best intentions, I can't keep myself from hoovering down the works. Fresh-cut, extra-crispy french fries (ideally with aioli) top my list, but I'll devour the tasty tubers mashed, baked, scalloped, gratinéed, or roasted. And when I want the most bang for my buck, I smash 'em.

6 tablespoons (90 mL) olive oil, divided
16 unpeeled baby potatoes, whole, or 4 unpeeled russet potatoes, quartered
⅓ cup (80 mL) finely chopped fresh basil (stems discarded)
4 cloves garlic, minced
Salt and freshly ground black pepper

Preheat grill to medium-high direct heat (see page 247).

In a large bowl, add 2 tablespoons (30 mL) of the olive oil and toss potatoes.

Grill potatoes for approximately 30 minutes, turning occasionally, or until cooked throughout and super-crispy on the outside (and when I say super-crispy, I mean browned and crisped to within an inch of their lives).

While potatoes are cooking, add remaining oil, garlic, and basil to the original bowl. Add roasted potatoes. Use a fork or any blunt instrument to smash potatoes. Do not smash so much that they are smooth. Toss thoroughly so that potatoes are coated with oil, basil, and spices, and let the heat unlock their flavors. Season to taste with salt and pepper.

yield Serves 4 as a side dish **active prep time** 10 minutes **grilling time** 30 minutes **advance work** Garlic, basil, and oil can be placed in bowl before guests arrive. After the potatoes are grilled, the only thing that remains to be done is the smashing. **oven version** Roast potatoes on the grill, or in a 400°F (200°C) oven for approximately 30 minutes, or until cooked throughout and super-crispy on the outside.

naked corn

There are many techniques for grilling corn. I've tried every option, and this method is by far the simplest.

4 ears corn, husked

Preheat grill to medium-high direct heat (see page 247). Grill the corn for 7 to 10 minutes. Every 2 minutes or so, roll each cob a quarter turn. The kernels should begin to brown in spots but should not be allowed to burn. Remove from grill and serve.

yield Serves 4 as a side dish **active prep time** 2 minutes **grilling time** 10 minutes **advance work** Corn can be husked earlier in the day.

spears of fire

Grilling asparagus miraculously transforms it from the vegetable you hated as a kid to a sweet, scrumptious treat that you can't get enough of as an adult.

1 pound (500 g) fresh asparagus (Look for thick, firm stalks with firm, deep green or purplish tips.)
¼ cup (60 mL) olive oil
1 teaspoon (5 mL) salt

Preheat grill to medium-high direct heat (see page 247).

Trim off the tough bottom ends of the spears by grasping each end and bending it gently until it snaps at its natural point of tenderness—usually two-thirds of the way down the spear. Or do it the fast way and cut all spears to a length of 6 inches (15 cm). (If the spear is less than 6 inches/15 cm long, chances are it has already been trimmed for you.) Then take a vegetable peeler and peel off the outer skin of the lower half of the remaining stalk.

Place asparagus on a plate. Drizzle oil overtop and roll spears until they are coated. Sprinkle with salt and turn again.

Grill asparagus for 5 minutes over a hot grill. Each minute or so, roll each spear a quarter turn. The asparagus should begin to brown in spots (indicating that its natural sugars are caramelizing) but should not be allowed to char. Dripping oil may cause flare-ups. Keep a glass or spray bottle of water handy to spritz on coals if necessary.

Remove from grill and serve (eating spears with your fingers enhances the experience).

yield Serves 4 as a side dish **active prep time** 10 minutes **grilling time** 5 minutes **advance work** Spears can be trimmed and peeled earlier in the day. Store upright in water. Can also be grilled before guests arrive and served at room temperature. **pan version** Oiled and salted spears can be pan-seared over medium-high heat for approximately 5 minutes. Each minute or so, roll spears a quarter turn.

mambo chicken

The lime juice and tamari sauce in this marinade are natural tenderizers that butter up the chicken—allowing the garlic and fresh ginger to move in for the kill. Top it all off with the sweet heat of a fresh mango salsa, and you've got a simple, succulent meal that's full of flava.

mambo chicken

3 cloves garlic, minced
One 2-inch (5 cm) knob of fresh ginger, peeled and grated
3 tablespoons (45 mL) tamari or soy sauce
3 tablespoons (45 mL) freshly squeezed lime juice
1½ tablespoons (22.5 mL) toasted sesame oil
½ teaspoon (2 mL) salt
½ teaspoon (2 mL) freshly ground black pepper
8 boneless skin-on chicken thighs or 4 boneless, skin-on chicken breasts

In a large bowl, combine garlic, ginger, tamari, lime juice, sesame oil, salt, and pepper.

Add the chicken and turn several times to mix the ingredients.

Cover and marinate for 2 hours in the refrigerator. Turn once or twice.

Preheat grill to medium-high direct heat.

Grill chicken for about 5 minutes per side, or until no pink remains.

Place the cooked chicken on warmed plates and spoon a generous serving of Mango Salsa overtop each serving.

mango salsa

2 ripe, fragrant mangoes, peeled, pitted, and cut in ¼-inch (6 mm) cubes
¼ cup (60 mL) freshly squeezed lime juice
½ cup (125 mL) coarsely chopped fresh cilantro (stems discarded), lightly packed
1 jalapeño or serrano chili (depending on your heat tolerance), seeds and membranes
    discarded, chopped finely
3 green onions, finely sliced

Combine all the ingredients in a medium bowl and mix thoroughly with a fork. Reserve.

yield 4 servings **level of difficulty** As easy as grilling chicken. **active prep time** 20 minutes **inactive prep time** 2 hours **grilling time** 15 minutes **advance work** Salsa can be made earlier in the day. Chicken can be marinated earlier in the day and left in the marinade. **oven/pan version** Chicken can be pan-seared over medium-high heat, or broiled, for approximately 5 minutes per side. **music to cook by** Spanish Harlem Orchestra, *United We Swing*. This large ensemble of Latin jazz veterans is keeping the salsa tradition alive and kicking. **liquid assets** Get your mojo workin' with a mojito.

grilled pizza boot camp

SHORT OF MOVING TO NAPLES, ITALY, nothing can elevate the quality of your pizza-eating existence more than learning how to grill pizza on your own backyard BBQ. I am so addicted to this technique that a few years ago I cowrote *Pizza on the Grill* with my kindred culinary spirit Elizabeth Karmel. What makes the pizzas so mind-blowing is that they take so little effort and so few tools to produce. The essence of grilled pizza is its life-changing crust: crispy, slightly charred, and smoky. And because the rustic flavor of a grilled pizza crust is bigger, bolder, and more textural than that of a traditionally baked pizza, it's a perfect base for a wide variety of nontraditional ingredients and flavors. Once you have mastered the basic steps of grilling the crust, and have knocked out a few simple pies, you can unleash your inner Leonardo da Vinci and create your own masterpiece.

Grilled pizza can be broken down into four key components: dough, sauce, toppings, and cheese. Paradoxically, even though grilling the dough is the most crucial step in making grilled pizza, just about any pizza dough can be transformed into a heavenly crust with the help of a generous splash of olive oil, a dusting of coarsely ground cornmeal, and the heat of your grill. Sure, you can make dough from scratch, but a buck or two will buy you a ball at your local pizza joint or grocery store. (If you live in Los Angeles and are lucky enough to live near a Pitfire Pizza location, my buddy and fellow pizzaholic David Sanfield will hook you up with *the crust you can trust*.) This will leave you with plenty of time to climb the food chain in search of fresh, flavorful ingredients for your sauce and toppings, and robust artisanal cheeses that will make *you* melt. Now that's *amore*!

the grill drill

BEFORE GETTING STARTED, assess your burner configuration and figure out how to set your grill for indirect heat. There are three common burner configurations for gas grills and one for charcoal grills:

- ☞ **two-burner grills** This configuration is found mostly in older grills. Because the heat source is coming from just one side, you may need to rotate the pizza 180 degrees halfway through the cooking process of both the dough and the topped pizza. Turn one burner off in step 7.

- ☞ **three-burner grills** For this style grill, you should stretch your dough so that it is twice as long as it is wide. Turn the middle burner off in step 7.

- ☞ **four-burner grills** (Fancy you!) Turn the middle two burners off in step 7.

- ☞ **charcoal grills** Let the coals get red hot, then gray-ashed. Move them to one side and follow the directions for a two-burner gas grill.

fire away

1. Remove the dough from the refrigerator and let it rise to room temperature, about an hour.

2. Prepare your toppings. The short time it takes to grill the pizza will only warm the toppings. Therefore, all toppings must either be edible raw—i.e., cured meats or olives—or be precooked. Set all your toppings on a tray by your BBQ so that you can have them at your fingertips when you start grilling.

3. Sprinkle your work surface with a handful of coarsely ground cornmeal. Use a rolling pin or wine bottle to roll out the dough thinly (³⁄₁₆ to ¼ inch/about 5 mm thick). Embrace the resulting organic shape. Brush both sides very generously with olive oil.

4. Preheat the grill with all the burners on high with the lid down for approximately 10 minutes, or until the internal temperature of the grill is at least 400°F (200°C). While the grill is preheating, roll out your dough.

5. Reset the grill to medium direct heat by turning all the burners to medium. Pick up the dough by the two corners closest to you. In one motion, lay it down flat—directly onto the cooking grate—from back to front as you would a tablecloth. I promise you the dough won't fall between the grates. Immediately close the lid and grill for 3 minutes (no peeking!). Then check the underside of the crust. If necessary, continue grilling until the bottom of the crust is well marked and nicely browned. And if it is browning unevenly, rotate before continuing to grill.

6. Use tongs to transfer the crust from the grill to a peel or rimless baking sheet. Close the lid to maintain the heat. Flip the crust to reveal the grilled side. Spread the entire surface with the sauce, add the toppings, and sprinkle with the cheese.

7. Reset the grill to high indirect heat by turning off the appropriate burners (see "the grill drill" on facing page) and increasing all remaining burners to high. Return the pizza to the grate over the unlit section, close the lid, and grill for approximately 7 to 10 minutes, or until the bottom is golden brown and the cheese is bubbly. Remove from the grill and serve immediately.

blistered corn and asparagus pizza

This is my all-time favorite pizza to make at home.

1 tablespoon (15 mL) butter
2 ears corn, husked, or 1 cup (250 mL) frozen corn, thawed
12 asparagus spears, trimmed and cut in ¼-inch (6 mm) slices
12 oil-packed sun-dried tomatoes, coarsely chopped
Salt and freshly ground black pepper
Chili pepper flakes
1 ball prepared pizza dough
¼ cup (60 mL) uncooked coarse cornmeal or uncooked polenta (for dusting dough)
Olive oil (for brushing dough)
1 cup (250 mL) basil pesto
6 ounces (175 g) brie, rind removed, cut in ¼-inch-thick (6 mm) strips, then cut in 1-inch
  (2.5 cm) squares

In a sauté pan over medium-high heat, add butter. When butter is melted, cut kernels from the cob directly into pan. Add asparagus. Sauté for approximately 5 minutes, or until corn shows signs of browning. Add sun-dried tomatoes, and the salt, pepper, and chili pepper flakes to taste. Reserve.

Follow steps 1 to 6 on page 141. After flipping crust in step 6, spread pesto over entire crust, distribute contents from sauté pan evenly over pesto, and top with brie cheese. Follow remaining directions in step 7.

yield 2–4 servings **uncommon goods** Coarsely ground cornmeal (often sold as polenta). **level of difficulty** You may burn through a few balls of dough learning to finesse the crust, but once you get the hang of it, it's like riding a bike. **active prep time** 15 minutes **grilling time** 15 minutes **shortcuts** Buy your dough. **advance work** Toppings can be sautéed up to a couple of hours in advance. **music to cook by** The Verve, *Urban Hymns*. Every bittersweet symphony should be followed by a grilled pizza. **liquid assets** Cru Beaujolais (such as Moulin-à-vent, Morgon, and Fleurie) is a poor man's fine burgundy. It is often more supple and made to drink young—which makes it a perfect complement for a pizza like this.

base sauces

onion marmalade base

2 tablespoons (30 mL) olive oil
1 tablespoon (15 mL) butter
3 large yellow onions, thinly sliced
1 teaspoon (5 mL) salt

Heat the oil and butter together in a large, heavy sauté pan over medium heat. When the butter bubbles, add the onions and salt, and cook, covered, for 20 minutes, stirring occasionally. Remove the cover and cook, stirring occasionally, until the onions are all a deep golden color, about 20 more minutes.

yield 1 cup (250 mL), enough for 1 pizza **advance work** Can be made up to 2 days in advance. **active prep time** 5 minutes **cooking time** 40 minutes

roasted garlic paste base

3 heads garlic
3 tablespoons (45 mL) olive oil (plus extra for drizzling)
Salt

Preheat oven to 400°F (200°C).

Remove the first layer of papery skin from the garlic. Slice off ¼ inch (6 mm) from the pointy tops. Place each head on a sheet of aluminum foil, cut side up. Drizzle with the oil and season with salt. Wrap each head in the foil and roast until the cloves are golden brown and soft, about 1 hour. Remove from the heat and let cool.

Remove the roasted cloves from their skins. The most efficient way to do this is to squeeze the whole head from the bottom directly into a bowl. Add the 3 tablespoons (45 mL) of oil and a pinch of salt. Use a whisk to vigorously combine into a paste.

yield About ½ cup (125 mL), enough for 1 pizza **advance work** Can be made up to 2 days in advance. **active prep time** 5 minutes **inactive cooking time** 1 hour

favorite combos

fire-roasted tomato & cabrales pizza

SAUCE 1 cup (250 mL) Onion Marmalade Base (see facing page)

TOPPING 1¼ cups (310 mL) oven-roasted cherry tomatoes

CHEESE 4 ounces (125 g) Cabrales or your favorite blue cheese, crumbled

magic mushroom medley pizza

SAUCE ½ cup (125 mL) Roasted Garlic Paste Base (see facing page)

TOPPINGS Sauté 1 diced leek with 10 ounces (300 g) of mixed wild mushrooms, some fresh thyme, and a generous splash of cognac

CHEESE 6 ounces (175 g) Camembert cheese, cut in ¼-inch-thick (6 mm) strips

puttanesca pizza

SAUCE 1 cup (250 mL) of your favorite tomato sauce

TOPPINGS 2 minced cloves garlic, ¼ teaspoon (1 mL) red chili pepper flakes, ½ cup (125 mL) pitted Niçoise olives, 2 tablespoons (30 mL) capers, and 6 anchovy fillets

CHEESE ¼ cup (60 mL) grated pecorino Romano cheese plus 1 cup (250 mL) grated Asiago cheese

eggplant caviar

To the best of my cloudy recollection, my dad only ever made three dishes: his legendary gaucho steak (see page 62), a grated tomato and olive oil concoction that he served alongside crusty bits of bread (long before bruschetta went mainstream), and this old-world Romanian recipe he learned from his father. It may appear simple, but it will transform any pedestrian eggplant into instant royalty.

2 whole eggplants (the big, fat variety as opposed to the Japanese variety)
¼ cup (60 mL) olive oil
Salt and freshly ground black pepper
Triangles of toasted caraway rye bread or your favorite flavorful crackers

Preheat grill to medium-high direct heat (see page 247).

Place whole eggplants, as is, on grill.

Rotate a quarter turn every 5 minutes for approximately 30 minutes, or until all of the skin is charred to a crisp and eggplants have popped, blown steam like a kettle, and shrunken in size by about one-third.

Let cool, then remove and discard skin. Place eggplant flesh in a bowl. Use a double-bladed chopper or close facsimile to chop into a fine mush. (A blender or food processor will purée the seeds—which is undesirable.)

Add oil, salt, and pepper, and blend thoroughly with a fork. Serve with your choice of crackers.

yield 2 cups (500 mL) **level of difficulty** Since the intent is to burn the eggplant to a crisp, it's virtually impossible to fail. **active prep time** 10 minutes **grilling time** 30 minutes **advance work** Can be made up to a day in advance. **music to cook by** Various artists, *Electric Gypsyland*. Modern remixes of great music from the Romani people.

glazed-over bananas

The USDA recommends two to four servings of fresh fruit a day. How you prepare it is your business.

2 tablespoons (30 mL) dark rum
2 tablespoons (30 mL) honey
1 teaspoon (5 mL) ground cinnamon
4 bananas
1 pint (500 mL) chocolate ice cream or frozen yogurt

Preheat grill to medium-high direct heat (see page 247).

In a small bowl, blend rum, honey, and cinnamon. Reserve.

Leaving their peel on, slice bananas in half lengthwise. Brush the cut sides with honey-rum mixture.

Grill bananas, cut side down, for 3 minutes, or until bananas develop visible grill marks.

Turn bananas and brush again generously with honey-rum mixture. Continue grilling, with lid down, for 5 minutes, or until bananas are browned on top, cooked throughout, and beginning to separate from the peels.

Serve with ice cream.

yield 4 servings level of difficulty A monkey (with a grill) could make this. active prep time 10 minutes grilling time 10 minutes advance work Honey-rum mixture can be made a day in advance. music to cook by Jónsi, Go. A stunningly uplifting album from the lead singer of Iceland's Sigur Rós.

happy endings

desserts

When my parents took me out to buffets as a child, I would pick away at a few morsels of the savory stuff, then wear out a path to the dessert table. Ironically, I never developed a taste for making desserts. In fact, when I wrote my first cookbook, I dodged the whole dessert bullet by compiling a list of 10 Ways to Avoid Making Dessert. A few years later, I circumvented the issue again by creating a sequel to the list for *The Surreal Gourmet Entertains*. Since then, I've slowly weaned myself off store-bought desserts. What follows are a few of my favorites.

pyrotechnic pineapple

It's always impressive to see flames leap out of a pan and lick the ceiling of a restaurant kitchen. But the pyrotechnics are not just for show. Burning alcohol intensifies the inherent flavors of whatever is in the pan. It's easier than it looks to flambé like a professional chef. And nothing demonstrates your prowess in the kitchen or ignites a passionate end to a romantic dinner like confidently controlling a four-alarm blaze in a sizzling pan of perfectly caramelized pineapple.

1 ripe pineapple
3 tablespoons (45 mL) butter
4 tablespoons (60 mL) granulated sugar, divided
2 ounces (60 mL) Grand Marnier, Cointreau, or dark rum
2 scoops vanilla ice cream or frozen yogurt

Before flambéing, see Fire Regulations (page 249).

Sit the pineapple on its side, and slice it in half vertically through the leafy section (see diagram page 255). Chisel out the core of each half and discard. Then cut around the fleshy sections with a knife (as you would a grapefruit). Remove flesh with a spoon and cut into small chunks. Reserve flesh and exterior shells.

Melt butter in a sauté pan over medium-high heat. Add pineapple chunks, but none of the juice, and stir occasionally for approximately 5 minutes, or until they begin to brown.

Sprinkle 1 tablespoon (15 mL) of sugar over the pineapple and stir for 1 minute, or until sugar has dissolved. Repeat the process, 1 tablespoon (15 mL) at a time, with the remaining sugar. Cook until pineapple and sugar are nicely browned.

Pour in Grand Marnier, let it heat up for 5 to 10 seconds, then ignite. The flames should jump about 2 feet (60 cm) high, then burn out after about 10 seconds (along with most of the alcoholic content).

Place a single scoop of ice cream in each of the hollowed-out pineapple shells and pour half of the contents of pan overtop each. Serve immediately with 2 spoons per couple.

yield 4 servings **le secret** Start with a ripe, fragrant pineapple. **level of difficulty** You must possess the capacity to light a match without fear. **active prep time** 15 minutes **advance work** Pineapple can be cut earlier in the day. **music to cook by** The Flaming Lips, *Yoshimi Battles the Pink Robots*. Psych-pop perfection featuring one of my all-time favorite tracks, "Do You Realize?"

s'more shooters

This rich, chocolaty indulgence is the NC-17 version of the campfire classic.

12 large marshmallows
1 cup (250 mL) half-and-half cream
½ pound (250 g) best-available-quality bittersweet chocolate, chopped in teeny-weeny bits
½ cup (125 mL) milk
¾ cup (185 mL) amaretto, divided
½ cup (125 mL) graham cracker crumbs

Twelve 3-ounce (90 mL) glasses

Toast marshmallows over a campfire or stovetop until golden brown. Let cool and reserve.

In a small pot, bring half-and-half to a boil. In a medium bowl, add chocolate. Pour cream over chocolate and stir until chocolate has fully melted.

Return chocolate ganache to the pot and whisk in milk. Over medium heat, bring to a simmer and stir in ½ cup (125 mL) of the amaretto.

Pour remaining amaretto into a small bowl so that it is ¼ inch (6 mm) deep and place graham cracker crumbs on a small saucer.

To assemble, dip the rims of the glasses in amaretto, then in the graham cracker crumbs. Transfer hot chocolate to a pitcher or measuring cup, then pour into glasses. Top with a toasted marshmallow.

yield 12 shooters (it's hard to stop at one serving!) **uncommon goods** 3-ounce (90 mL) glasses **level of difficulty** Any camper can make these. **active prep time** 10 minutes **cooking time** 20 minutes **shortcuts** Don't bother toasting the marshmallows. **advance work** Hot chocolate can be made up to 2 days in advance. Marshmallows can be toasted, and glasses rimmed, earlier in the day. **music to cook by** Hot Chocolate, *Hot Chocolate*. A sexy dance party.

nutcases

In this one-bite cheese course, the pungent, slightly salty flavor of Gorgonzola is taunted by the sweetness of honey and the spiciness of the nuts. It will drive your taste buds crazy.

1 teaspoon (5 mL) granulated sugar
¼ teaspoon (1 mL) salt
⅛ teaspoon (0.5 mL) cayenne pepper
24 cosmetically perfect walnut halves (Select packages that say "halves," not "pieces.")
1 tablespoon (15 mL) canola oil
1 cup (250 mL) demerara sugar (for presentation)
6 ounces (175 g) Gorgonzola cheese, room temperature
3 tablespoons (45 mL) honey

20 walnuts in the shell (needed for their shells only)

Preheat oven to 350°F (180°C).

Insert a paring knife into the small opening at the top of each walnut shell and twist it to split the shell in half. (Don't hate me when some break into several pieces in all the wrong places. This is an inexact science and some walnuts are much more difficult to split evenly than others—hence the spare shells.) Clean out the nut casings, and eat the little walnut fragments. Reserve the empty shells.

In a small bowl, combine the granulated sugar, salt, and cayenne. In a medium bowl, toss walnut halves with oil. Sprinkle nuts with sugar mixture and toss thoroughly. Transfer nuts to a baking sheet and roast for 10 minutes, or until browned and toasted. Let cool to room temperature.

To assemble, spread demerara sugar on a plate and set walnut shells in sugar. Sandwich 1 teaspoon (5 mL) of cheese between 2 walnut halves. Then place mini walnut sandwiches upright in the walnut shells. Just before serving, drizzle honey overtop.

yield 12 bites **uncommon goods** Whole walnuts in their shells **level of difficulty** Like breaking into your own house: once you successfully crack the nut, there is nothing else to worry about. **active prep time** 25 minutes **cooking time** 10 minutes **shortcuts** Use store-bought spiced nuts and/or skip the whole shell-in-sugar deal and serve the cheese-stuffed nuts au naturel on a plate. **advance work** Whole nuts can be split anytime, and the walnut halves can be seasoned and roasted up to 2 days in advance; the assembly can be done hours in advance, except for the honey, which should be drizzled at the last second. **music to cook by** The Jesus and Mary Chain, *Psychocandy*. Just like honey—but with more feedback. **liquid assets** A Sauternes, a late harvest wine, an ice wine, or a port will all work magically in their own individual ways.

coffee crispée

Making creamy, sweet, custardy crème brûlée is a no-brainer—except for the tricky bit at the very end where you have to make like a welder and caramelize the sugar with a blowtorch. Fortunately, using your broiler instead can minimize the challenge.

6 egg yolks
8 tablespoons (120 mL) sugar, divided
2 tablespoons (30 mL) instant espresso or coffee powder (the freeze-dried stuff)
½ cup (125 mL) heavy cream, divided
½ teaspoon (2 mL) vanilla extract

Preheat oven to 300°F (150°C).

In a medium bowl, whisk egg yolks and 6 tablespoons (90 mL) of the sugar for 1 minute, or until smooth and pale yellow in color. Reserve.

In a second medium bowl, add espresso granules and ¼ cup (60 mL) of the cream. Whisk until smooth, then add remaining cream and the vanilla, and whisk until well blended.

Very gently, fold espresso cream mixture into egg yolks.

Use a ladle to pour custard mixture into espresso cups, filling them three-fourths of the way to the top.

Place cups in a baking dish or roasting pan and transfer to oven. Fill a pitcher with warm tap water. Before closing oven door, pour water into pan (but not into the cups themselves!) until it reaches halfway up the sides of the cups.

Bake for 40 minutes, or until the custards jiggle just slightly when you shake the pan. Remove pan from oven and leave out on counter, allowing the residual heat of the water to finish the cooking process.

When custards have fully solidified, refrigerate for 2 hours.

Just before serving, sprinkle ½ teaspoon (2 mL) of sugar evenly overtop each custard. Use a small blowtorch to caramelize the sugar. Alternatively, place cups 1 inch (2.5 cm) below oven broiler under a watchful eye for approximately 2 minutes, or until sugar caramelizes.

yield 12 servings **uncommon goods** espresso cups, blowtorch **level of difficulty** True, you have to make like a welder, but you don't have to do it while balancing on a steel beam. **active prep time** 25 minutes **inactive prep time** 2 hours **cooking time** 40 minutes **shortcuts** Skip dessert. **advance work** Custards can be made up to 2 days in advance. Caramelizing the sugar must be done at the last minute. **music to cook by** Peggy Lee, *Black Coffee*, is absolute torch, no twang. **liquid assets** Hard-core caffeine junkies should serve with a demitasse of real espresso.

maple bacon–crunch
ice cream

In the fourth season of *Glutton for Punishment*, I traveled with my four-person crew of fellow adventurers to Austin, Texas, for the Austin Ice Cream Festival's ice-cream-making competition. I had never made ice cream before in my life, but under the expert tutelage of Amy Simmons of Amy's Ice Creams and Cristiana Ginatta of Paciugo Gelato, I there learned how to make a classic base and create my own flavors from scratch. That's when the real fun started.

I tested several flavor combinations that appealed to me: a jacked-up version of Ben & Jerry's classic Chunky Monkey that I made with roasted bananas; a dark-chocolate and chipotle blend; and durian, the unbearably stinky fruit I had recently fallen in love with in Asia. But the flavor I created that got the most votes from my test audiences—and ultimately won me first place—was Maple Bacon–Crunch. It's hard to argue with crisp, smoky bacon, encased in brittle and surrounded by the richness of real maple ice cream. This union of quintessentially Canadian ingredients may sound incongruous at first—but clearly they are a winning combination.

maple ice cream

5 egg yolks
Pinch of salt
½ cup (125 mL) granulated sugar
2 cups (500 mL) whole milk
2 cups (500 mL) maple syrup (ideally grade B)
4 cups (1 L) heavy cream

4 pounds (1.8 kg) rock salt for the ice-cream-making process (only if you are using an old-school crank, as I did)

In a medium bowl, add yolks, salt, and sugar. Whip until pale yellow.

Transfer to a large pot and stir in milk. Over medium heat, gently bring mixture to a scald (the point just before a simmer at which a film forms over the back of a metal spoon that is dipped into the liquid).

Remove from heat and add maple syrup. Chill liquid in refrigerator for 30 minutes.

Stir in cream and transfer to an ice-cream maker. Follow manufacturer's directions.

(continued . . .)

(. . . continued)

to finish

When ice cream is ready, stir in about a cup (250 mL) of Bacon Brittle bits. (It's your call on how much to add.) Transfer to a container with a lid and freeze for a minimum of 2 hours before serving.

bacon brittle (a.k.a. pig candy)

This improved version of the brittle I made for the competition is based on a recipe from my friend Elizabeth Karmel. The recipe makes about 3 cups (750 mL), which allows for a generous amount of leftovers. I promise you they won't last for long.

6 strips smoky bacon (my favorite national brand is Nueske's)
2 cups (500 mL) granulated sugar
2 tablespoons (30 mL) butter (plus extra for greasing the pan)
1 teaspoon (5 mL) baking soda
¼ teaspoon (1 mL) ground dried chipotle or a pinch of cayenne pepper

Set out a cookie sheet and grease it with butter. Reserve.

Cook bacon, any way you want, until it is super-crispy. Pat dry with a paper towel. Let cool, then chop as finely as possible (think: dust). Reserve.

In a saucepan over medium-high heat, add sugar. Stir constantly for approximately 4 minutes, or until sugar melts into a light golden liquid. (If lumps develop, remove from heat temporarily and keep stirring. They will melt away.) Keep stirring for approximately 2 more minutes, or until liquid turns the color of butterscotch. Remove from heat and immediately stir in butter. Then add baking soda and mix thoroughly. Stir in bacon and chipotle. Pour onto cookie sheet and let cool until hard (approximately 15 minutes).

Use a mallet or your hands to break into bite-size pieces. Then smash about one-third of the brittle into itsy-bitsy pieces. Use the small bits for your ice cream and store remaining Pig Candy in an airtight jar. Guard with your life.

yield About 2 quarts (2 L) of ice cream and 3 cups (750 mL) of Bacon Brittle **uncommon goods** An ice-cream maker **level of difficulty** Moderately difficult. And if you have an old-school, hand-cranked machine, it's like a 20-minute workout on an elliptical machine. **storability** Over time, the Pig Candy will dissolve into the ice cream. If you have lots of willpower and don't intend to eat all the ice cream you make immediately, store the Pig Candy separately and crumble over ice cream just before serving. **active prep time** 1 hour **inactive prep time** 45 minutes **shortcuts** Buy a pint of Ben & Jerry's. **advance work** Can be made days in advance. **music to churn by** "O Canada"

dirty, rotten, stinky cheeses and the wines that love them

IF THE THOUGHT OF CHEESE conjures up images of a prefab tray, piled high with unidentifiable cubes in various shades of yellow and a token wedge of brie, it's time to wake up and smell the aromas. There's a universe of cheese out there that will either completely disgust you—or change your life. That's right, I'm talking about stinky cheeses—bacterial mutations covered in festering mold. The kind that if you get them just ripe enough will ooze like slime and make your dirty socks smell like the latest Calvin Klein fragrance by comparison. In other words, cheese nirvana.

Like a glistening pearl in a barnacle-covered oyster shell, stinky cheeses offer a gastronomic bonanza to those who can get past their initial appearance—and, of course, their overwhelming fumes. The reward for persevering is a pleasingly funky taste sensation that saturates every last taste bud with a robust, tangy fusion of flavors. I was inducted into the world of stinky *fromage* during a wine pilgrimage to Bordeaux. In no time, I started neglecting the elaborate multicourse meals in order to save room for the cheese service that inevitably follows every grandiose French meal. Years later, my true stinky-cheese epiphany happened at Mraz & Sohn, a restaurant in Vienna, Austria. After a sumptuous meal, I wandered over to the cheese cart to survey the odiferous delicacies. Half jokingly, I asked the waitress where the really, really stinky cheeses were. Without missing a beat, she pulled out a drawer to reveal a holy grail of mold-covered, runny cheeses. The motley assemblage looked as threatening as it did appealing, and anyone with an acute sense of smell would have beaten a hasty retreat. But I stared in amazement and asked for a taste of each, along with a glass of Penfolds Bin 389 Cabernet-Shiraz (her recommendation). The gloriously pungent French cheeses, alongside a wine that was exploding with ripe, supple fruit, created a spine-tingling culinary orgasm.

In my never-ending quest to live well beyond my means, I set out to learn why the artisan cheeses they eat in Europe are so different from what we have all grown to accept as cheese in North America.

I soon learned that the nose-numbing smell and moldy rind that are the hallmarks of a stinky cheese are the result of polycultures and bacteria that form on the outer skin of the cheese as it ripens. As it is aged, the cheese skin absorbs the earthiness of the damp cellars, and the mold that develops on the rind, called *bacillus linens*, generates an ammonia-like smell. Some of the finished cheeses are also "washed" in locally produced spirits, such as Marc, a rough Burgundian brandy, which ferments the natural fats and adds another layer of complexity to the already heady aromas.

Another element contributes to the difference between European and American cheeses—although there are dissenting opinions about its importance. In America, most cheeses are required by law to be pasteurized, a process that heats the milk to 161°F (72°C) degrees, and kills the potentially dangerous bacteria (and unfortunately some of the flavor). In France, where the cheese is not required to be pasteurized, the milk is heated to a lower temperature, which preserves the integrity of the raw ingredients. Of course, the quality of the milk itself, which is determined by what the cows graze upon, is also a key factor. Then there is the issue of making cheese to suit the taste of the consumer. European cheeses are crafted to meet European tastes, which tend to be bolder and less convenience-driven. Most of the French cheeses imported to America, such as familiar foil-wrapped soft-cheese wedges and run-of-the-mill brie, conform to American regulations *and* tastes. This double fault produces much milder cheeses. They may be French, but they are not *Frrrench*.

There is no question that stinky cheese is an acquired taste. But if you ignore what your nose is telling you and take the leap, you may never eat a pedestrian cube of cheese again.

> To heighten the aromas and supple textures of your cheeses, remove them from the refrigerator a minimum of two hours before serving and let rise to room temperature. I often leave cheeses out on my counter for a couple of days to allow them to mature to their ultimate pungency.

my ultimate cheese list

époisse My all-time favorite cheese. This soft, Burgundian cow's milk gem may smell like dirty socks and sweaty armpits, but it tastes like heaven. Le Cados and Camembert au Calvados, both from Normandy, and Ami du Chambertin from Burgundy are slightly more approachable variations on a theme of Époisse.

stilton Looks like (and is!) a cheese that has been left in a dark, dank cellar and injected with mold. Tastes rich and creamy.

cabrales A Spanish version of Stilton, but way more intense.

chèvre noir This two- to three-year-old goat's milk cheddar from Quebec comes wrapped in black wax. Amazing in sandwiches, in salads, or on its own.

aged gouda Young Gouda is swell, but the stuff that has been aged for five or more years has notes of caramel that will blow your mind.

comté An aged Gruyère from France with an intense nutty flavor.

chèvre affiné A loglike, six-month-old goat cheese with a gamey flavor.

wine and stinky cheese pairing

WHEN FIRST I WROTE THE STORY OF MY CHEESE EPIPHANY—several years and many, many rounds of cheese ago—I pontificated about pairing cheeses with big reds. Now I have switched allegiances and am all about the whites. My favorite wines to drink with stinky cheeses are dessert wines (Sauternes and other late harvest wines, ice wines, and ice ciders), sweet German Rieslings (Auslese and Spätlese), and big aromatic whites such as Gewürztraminers, Viogniers, and rich Chardonnays. If you do choose to serve red wine with your cheese, go for big reds with strong tannins.

20 ways to avoid making dessert

IF YOU LOVE DESSERTS but don't have the time or the inclination to make them, here is an updated version of my original 20 Ways to Avoid Making Dessert.

1. Serve an assortment of penny candy.

2. Serve someone else's homemade brownies.

3. Top premium ice cream with fresh strawberries, raspberries, blueberries, mangoes, kiwis, or figs.

4. Top any of the preceding ice-cream combinations with a tablespoon (15 mL) of flaming Grand Marnier, Cointreau, sambuca, or dark rum.

5. Serve frozen ice-cream treats.
    OLD SCHOOL: Fudgsicles, Creamsicles, or Popsicles
    NEW SCHOOL: Häagen-Dazs, Dove, or Ben & Jerry's bars
    ADVENTURE CLUB: Hire an ice-cream truck to swing by after dinner.

6. Serve fortune cookies.
    ADVENTURE CLUB: Pull out the fortunes with tweezers and replace them with your own prophecies.

7. Serve a selection of exotic fruits.

8. Let guests make their own s'mores.

9. Spike coffee with your favorite liqueur.

10. Pour a dessert wine or port.

11. Top vanilla or chocolate ice cream with a tablespoon (15 mL) of crème de menthe liqueur and serve with chocolates, and/or grate white or dark chocolate overtop.

12. Serve a selection of very ripe cheeses with fancy fruit and nut crisps.

13. Dole out chocolate-covered espresso beans one at a time.

14. Serve Oreos and milk.

15. Open a box of chocolate truffles.

16. Bake frozen-dough cookies and serve them hot out of the oven.
    ADVENTURE CLUB: Pretend they are homemade and see if you can get away with it.

17. Open a box of Pepperidge Farm Pirouettes.

18. Melt a chocolate fondue.

19. Let them eat cake.

20. Have sex instead.

breakfast
of champions

breakfasts

During the week, I do my best to eat healthy breakfasts. I usually gravitate to the standard yogurt/granola/fruit fix— albeit with homemade granola and goat's milk yogurt. But on the weekend, I am all about pulling out the stops and whipping up a breakfast made from equal parts excess, indulgence, and hedonism.

banana french toastwich

Some recipes are born from brilliance—and some are happy accidents. Recently I was presenting my Banana French Toastwich recipe at Toronto's Good Food Festival. When I reached for the milk on my preset tray of ingredients, I realized my food wrangler had forgotten to buy it. I was about to throw in the towel and move on to my next recipe when someone in the audience shouted out that a stand just down the aisle was sampling chocolate milk. Crazy, I thought—yet oddly appealing. And while I am at it, why not take it over the top with a schmear of the cashew butter that was being sampled at the booth next door? At least it will be entertaining. To my amazement, the improvised French toast made the original pale in comparison. *Vive la banana république!*

4 eggs
½ cup (125 mL) chocolate milk
1 teaspoon (5 mL) ground cinnamon (plus extra to sprinkle on finished plate)
4 slices of multigrain bread or any other sliced bread
2 bananas, peeled and sliced
¼ cup (60 mL) cashew, almond, or peanut butter (smooth or crunchy)
2 tablespoons (30 mL) butter
½ cup (125 mL) maple syrup

Beat eggs, chocolate milk, and cinnamon in a shallow bowl. Soak bread slices in egg mixture until completely soggy. Reserve on a plate.

Carefully spread 1 slice of soaked bread with 2 tablespoons (30 mL) of cashew butter. Cover with banana, then top with a second slice of bread (like a drippy banana sandwich). Reserve and repeat.

In a sauté pan, over medium to medium-high heat, melt butter. When butter is bubbling, add toastwiches. Cover pan with lid. Cook until golden brown on both sides and cooked throughout (approximately 4 minutes on the first side and 3 minutes on the second side). The object is to brown the outside nicely and cook the inside thoroughly without drying it out. Make an incision in the middle to test for doneness. If the outside is done but the inside is still runny, reduce heat to medium-low and cover for a couple more minutes.

Remove toastwiches from pan and place on warmed plates. Remove pan from burner, carefully wipe out browned butter with a paper towel, then immediately add maple syrup to pan for 15 seconds. Pour warmed syrup over toastwiches.

yield 2 servings **uncommon goods** Cashew butter **level of difficulty** Easy . . . albeit somewhat messy. **active prep time** 10 minutes **cooking time** 10 minutes **grown-up alternative** Those of you who do not live in a state of suspended adolescence can replace the chocolate milk with whole or 2% milk, and leave out the cashew butter. **music to cook by** Benoît Charest, *Triplets of Belleville* soundtrack. Uplifting morning music. **liquid assets** Mimosas

lassi come home

I always look forward to reading *SAVEUR* magazine's Top 100, which comes out every January. On occasion I send away for some of the ingredients on the list that are championed by the editors. I still have a few drops of the rose syrup from Italy that they recommended four years ago, and I dole it out to my friends by the thimbleful. A few years back, *SAVEUR* recommended a mango purée from India. (The brand was Rayna.)

Mango happens to be my desert-island fruit, but depending on the source and the season, fresh ones can vary between disappointing and intoxicating. The unadulterated canned version is consistently as good as the best mangoes I have ever tasted. Now I can make my own version of lassi, the classic Indian-style smoothie, all year round.

1 ripe banana
1 cup (250 mL) mango purée or 1 ripe, fragrant mango, peeled and pitted
¾ cup (185 mL) plain yogurt
1 tablespoon (15 mL) roughly chopped or grated fresh ginger (optional)
6 cubes ice

Add all ingredients to a blender and blend on high speed until smooth.

yield 2 great starts to the day **uncommon goods** Canned mango purée **level of difficulty** If you can operate a blender, you can make this. **active prep time** 5 minutes **music to blend by** Various artists, *Slumdog Millionaire* soundtrack

parking lot eggs

One of my favorite memories of the original Toastermobile tour (see page 10) was emerging bleary-eyed from my motel room in the morning, staggering through the parking lot to the Toastermobile, and whipping up a pan of eggs for my crew. Unable to muster the energy required to make a fluffy omelet, I simply scrambled the lot with whatever ingredients and leftovers I could scavenge from the refrigerator. No fuss, no muss—all flavor. I called them Parking Lot Eggs. The ingredients always change, but the name stuck.

10 eggs
Salt and lots of freshly ground black pepper (to taste)
½ cup (125 mL) (about 2 ounces/60 g) freshly grated Parmigiano
    Reggiano or whatever cheese is available
1 tablespoon (15 mL) olive oil
½ pound (250 g) pancetta, prosciutto, bacon, or ham, sliced crosswise
    in ¼-inch (6 mm) strips
6 green onions, finely chopped
1 jalapeño or serrano chili, seeds and membranes discarded, minced, or
    a pinch of ground dried chipotle
2–4 cloves garlic, minced
1 handful fresh cilantro, Italian parsley, or other herbs, stems discarded
1 ripe avocado, pitted and peeled then diced in ¼-inch (6 mm) cubes;
    and/or 1 cup (250 mL) of canned or jarred roasted red bell peppers

In a bowl, beat eggs, salt, pepper, and Parmigiano Reggiano. Reserve.

In a sauté pan over medium-high heat, add oil and cook pancetta, stirring occasionally until it starts getting crispy.

Add green onions, jalapeño, and garlic. Cook for 2 to 3 minutes, or until garlic shows the first sign of turning golden.

Add cilantro and avocado (and/or roasted peppers). Stir for 1 more minute.

Reduce heat to medium, add egg mixture to pan, and stir until eggs are cooked to your liking.

yield 4 servings **level of difficulty** Like making an omelet without worrying about how it looks. **active prep time** 10 minutes **cooking time** 10 minutes **advance work** The pancetta, onions, jalapeño, and garlic can be sautéed up to a few hours in advance. Eggs and cheese can be beaten a few hours in advance. **music to cook by** Lucinda Williams, *Car Wheels on a Gravel Road*. The official album of the Toastermobile tour.

blackened home fries from hell

Whenever I see home fries or hash browns on the menu of a breakfast joint, my mind conjures up images of crispy, picture perfect, golden brown potatoes. Inevitably my eggs arrive with a mound of snow-white, mealy spuds, offering only a teasing hint of the texture I yearn for. If they have any color at all, it is usually due to a deceptive dusting of paprika. Making crispy home fries takes a lot of patience and surface space—which is exactly why most busy restaurants are incapable of satisfying my craving. The beauty of cooking home fries at home is that you can brown (or blacken) them to your heart's content.

2 pounds (1 kg) potatoes (Yukon golds are my favorites, but any potato will work.)
a whole lotta butter
a whole lotta olive oil
6 cloves garlic, coarsely chopped
1 medium cooking onion, diced
¼ cup (60 mL) fresh rosemary, thyme, or dill (stems discarded)
Salt and freshly ground black pepper

Quarter potatoes with the skin on and steam, boil, or bake them until tender to the poke of a fork. Reserve.

In your best large nonstick pan, or well-seasoned skillet, over medium-high heat, add 1 tablespoon (15 mL) butter and 1 tablespoon (15 mL) olive oil. When the butter-oil mixture is hot, transfer potatoes to pan and use a spatula to chop the quarters into smaller pieces (there is no science here). As the potatoes absorb the butter and oil during cooking, continue to add in equal amounts, as required, to keep the pan well greased. Sauté for 20 minutes, turning occasionally, or until potatoes begin browning on all sides. If the potatoes start burning before they brown, reduce the heat.

Add garlic and onion and continue cooking for 15 more minutes, or until potatoes, garlic, and onion are all very browned and crispy.

When potatoes are almost done to your liking, add herbs, salt, and pepper to taste. Cook for a few more minutes, then serve immediately.

yield 4–6 servings le secret It's all in the timing of adding the garlic and onions (which can really be learned only through trial and error). Adding them too soon will cause them to burn before the potatoes are crisp, and too late will prevent the garlic and onion from fully caramelizing. level of difficulty Easy active prep time 5 minutes inactive prep time 30 minutes cooking time 40 minutes advance work Potatoes can be steamed, boiled, or baked, and then refrigerated up to a day in advance.

toast

1 bottle of chilled champagne or sparkling wine
2 glasses, ideally flutes (plus 1 glass for each additional person)
1 personal or global sentiment

Remove foil.

Point bottle away from anyone you truly care about, and remove the wire cage.

Drape a small towel over the top of the bottle and grip the cork firmly. Turn the bottle slowly and ease cork out.

Gracefully pour champagne into glasses.

Make eye contact, clink glasses, and express heartfelt sentiments.

yield 6 servings **adventure club** See photos

flip, flop, or fly?
my quest to break a guinness world record

Many of the episode ideas for *Glutton for Punishment* originated as jokes, dares, or farfetched suggestions that evolved into actual episodes over time. One such idea was to try and break an existing food-related Guinness World Record. This idea didn't really seem that wacked until our research revealed the sheer magnitude of the existing records. The world's largest omelet contained 60,000 eggs—and it only gets crazier. By the time we fully grasped what we were getting ourselves into, it was too late to back out. We had already pitched the episode concept to the Food Network—and they loved it.

After sifting through all of the biggest, fastest, and longest food categories, Vera, my fabulous, ball-busting, Russian-Israeli producer, suggested that I should try to break the current record for the most pancakes made in an hour.

"At least the record is in the hundreds, not thousands," she rationalized.

"But I've never made pancakes for more than six," I replied.

"Perfect," she said in her Russian accent. "Maybe you'll fail."

And before I knew it, I was on a plane to Calgary, Alberta.

Every summer, the entire city of Calgary is transformed into a giant playground as the Stampede takes over. Everybody gets into the action and virtually everywhere you look you see former civilians dressed in full cowboy regalia. In fact, it is illegal to walk down certain streets without wearing a 10-gallon hat (or at least that's what the mock judge will tell you before fining you and selling you one).

Necessity is the mother of invention. With a liquor law variance that allows many bars to stay open until the wee hours during the Stampede, it's not surprising that a hearty breakfast is required to recover from the former night's revelry and provide the energy for the next cycle of nonstop partying. During the 10 days of what the city bills as the "greatest outdoor show on earth," volunteers serve up an estimated 200,000 free pancakes to help fuel the romping rodeo spectacle. There was certainly no shortage of opportunity to practice my technique.

Once I realized how seriously Calgarians take their pancakes, I began to develop what can best be described as pancake performance anxiety. To add to the pressure, a Guinness adjudicator was flying in from New York City. His job was to ensure that I adhered to the Guinness World Record's stringent set of competitive rules—rules that are so strict that only three percent of all record-breaking attempts end successfully. In the pancake-making category, every pancake has to measure at least five inches in diameter, be no more than one centimeter high, and appear edible. And if that wasn't enough pressure, the *Calgary Herald* ran a front-page story about my world record attempt, which read: "TV STAR HOPES TO FLIP FLAPJACK RECORD." I could already visualize what the next day's

self-esteem-shattering headline would read if I failed in my quest: "TV STAR FLOPS IN FLAPJACK FLIPPING ATTEMPT."

In order to break the previous record set by a Denver-based caterer who claims to flip a million pancakes a year, I deconstructed every component of the pancake-making process and tried to streamline each step. I started by playing with the fat/sugar ratio in the batter so that it would cook faster, but burn slower. Then I tested a variety of pouring methods (batter dispensers are not sanctioned by the Guinness organization), and fussed over grill temperatures. I also customized my spatula by grinding an inch off the end and beveling the edges to a razor-sharp finish so that it would slide underneath the cakes with a minimum of resistance. I even tested different shoes to determine which style gave me the best traction.

As the sun rose over Rope Square on the big day, a group of curious gingham-clad rodeo enthusiasts ringed my grills. At precisely 8 a.m., a bullet was fired in the air, Wild West–style, and I ladled, flipped, and flapped my way faster than a bull shakes a rookie rider. Though the odds were definitely stacked against me, I surged in the final minutes, besting the previous record of 555 pancakes by four. I was left with a case of carpal flipping syndrome and a newfound appreciation for the humble pancake. And I can proudly say that my name is in the 2010 Guinness Book of World Records. How did I celebrate? With a short stack and a Guinness World Record–worthy number of Bloody Caesars.

yes pe-can! pancakes

Unlike the version I made in my quest for the Guinness World Record, these pancakes are built for comfort, not for speed.

½ cup (125 mL) pecan pieces
1½ cups (375 mL) all-purpose flour
¼ cup (60 mL) granulated sugar
1½ teaspoons (7.5 mL) baking powder
½ teaspoon (2 mL) salt
2 eggs
1½ cups (375 mL) buttermilk or whole milk
3 tablespoons (45 mL) butter, melted (plus extra for cooking)
¼–½ cup (60–125 mL) candied ginger, finely chopped
Zest of 1 orange
Maple syrup

Preheat oven to 350°F (180°C).

Set pecan pieces on a cookie sheet and bake for 5 minutes, or until well toasted. Let cool. Reserve.

Mix flour, sugar, baking powder, and salt in a large bowl. In a medium bowl, mix eggs, buttermilk, and melted butter. Slowly whisk wet ingredients into dry bowl. Do not overmix. Add additional buttermilk or flour, if necessary, to get it to that classic pancake-batter consistency. Let rest for 15 minutes so that the baking powder can work its magic and aerate the batter. Just before dropping pancakes, gently fold in ginger, pecans, and zest.

Pour maple syrup into a small pot and warm it over low heat.

Melt 1 tablespoon (15 mL) butter in a large pan over medium-high heat. When butter is sizzling, ladle batter to form pancakes. Once bubbles begin to form over the entire top of the pancakes and the bottom is golden brown, flip and continue cooking until second side is golden brown. Top with maple syrup. Repeat.

yield 4–6 servings uncommon goods Candied ginger adventure club For even fluffier pancakes, separate the egg whites from the yolks. Add the yolks at the point where the whole eggs are originally called for. Beat the whites to firm peaks and gently fold into the batter just before you are ready to drop it into the pan. level of difficulty Just a few steps more involved than making pancakes from a mix. active prep time 15 minutes inactive active prep time 15 minutes cooking time 10 minutes shortcuts Buy toasted pecan pieces. advance work Batter can be made up to 2 hours in advance. music to cook by Queen, "We Are the Champions." They will rock you. liquid assets Toast (see page 177).

and now for something completely surreal

edible illusions

There was nothing surreal about any of the food in my first cookbook. The title, *The Surreal Gourmet*, which I also adapted as my nom de plume, was inspired by the Dalí- and Magritte-influenced illustrations I painted to accompany my bachelor repertoire of recipes.

I had never even contemplated the type of dishes that have evolved into my signature style. But a fortuitous thing happened when the book came out: an Australian food critic, who took my moniker literally, chastised me for not presenting food that lived up to its surreal billing. My first reaction was to cry foul. After all, did the Galloping Gourmet really gallop? Did Jamie Oliver bare all when he was the Naked Chef?

The reviewer's words lingered in my mind until I had an epiphany: instead of wallowing in self-pity, I should revel in the opportunity. He had actually handed me the keys to a far more interesting world—one that no one else had explored. My first stab at surreal presentation was a rudimentary dessert made from a sculpted slice of cheesecake and an apricot half, which looked like a sunny-side-up egg. I graduated to dollops of brightly colored vegetables served on a painter's palette. Soon I was hooked.

I have since developed scores of surreal meals. But these whimsical presentations are only successful if the flavors follow through on the visual joke. That's why I've abandoned many more ideas than I've executed. When it all comes together, though, it's like hitting a Vegas jackpot.

lamb cupcakes

This is my go-to recipe for the surreal meals I do around the world. In some situations, due to local tastes or dietary restrictions, I have replaced the lamb with other meats such as confit duck leg or braised beef cheeks. The result is always an intensely meaty, wine-friendly dish that never fails to confuse and amuse.

4 lamb shanks
Salt and freshly ground black pepper
¼ cup (60 mL) all-purpose flour
7 tablespoons (105 mL) canola oil, divided
2 onions, chopped, divided
2 carrots, peeled and sliced
2 stalks celery, sliced
4 cups (1 L) chicken stock
½ bottle dry red wine
8 sprigs fresh rosemary, divided
6 sprigs fresh thyme
1 medium red beet
½ head garlic, chopped
2 eggs
1 cup (250 mL) breadcrumbs or panko
3 medium russet potatoes, peeled and quartered
¼ cup (60 mL) half-and-half cream, room temperature
¼ cup (60 mL) butter, room temperature

Muffin tin
8 cupcake liners
Vegetable oil spray

suggested prep order

Start by braising lamb.

Prepare lamb fixin's, potatoes, and roast beet while the shanks are braising.

cupcakes

Preheat oven to 300°F (150°C).

Season lamb shanks with salt and pepper. Roll in flour. In a large sauté pan over medium-high heat, add 3 tablespoons (45 mL) of oil. Add the lamb shanks and sear on all sides (about 2 minutes per side). Reserve.

(continued . . .)

(. . . continued)

In another sauté pan over medium heat, add 2 tablespoons (30 mL) oil and sauté half the onions, plus the carrots and celery, for approximately 6 minutes, or until they just begin to brown.

Add chicken stock to the veggie pan, stir up the brown bits off the bottom of the pan, and bring stock to a boil.

Transfer lamb shanks to a roasting pan, pour wine overtop. Pour entire contents of veggie pan overtop of lamb, spread half of the rosemary and all thyme overtop, and tightly seal the whole lot with foil.

Braise shanks in oven for approximately 3 to 4 hours, or until the lamb is falling-off-the-bone tender.

While lamb is braising, toss beet, as is, into oven. Cook for approximately 90 minutes, or until soft to the firm press of a thumb. Reserve.

Heat 2 tablespoons (30 mL) oil in a large, heavy sauté pan over medium heat. Add remaining onion and the garlic. Stir occasionally for approximately 20 minutes, or until they are browned to within an inch of their lives. Reserve.

When lamb is finished, strain off the braising juices. Let settle for 5 minutes, then separate the fat from the remaining juices and discard the fat. Transfer juices to a small pot over high heat and reduce by about three-quarters until it is thick like a demi-glace. Reserve.

After shanks have cooled, pull all the meat off the bones, discard any fat and gristle, and tear the remaining meat into small pieces.

Stem remaining rosemary and chop finely. Add to a large bowl along with eggs. Beat the eggs, then add the meat, 1/3 cup (80 mL) demi-glace, caramelized onions and garlic, and breadcrumbs. Mix thoroughly with a fork. Reserve. At this point meat mixture can be refrigerated for up to a couple of days.

icing

Steam potatoes over boiling water until tender to the poke of a fork.

Use a ricer, food mill, or standard-issue fork to mash potatoes. In a medium glass or metal bowl, blend the potatoes with cream and butter, and season to taste with salt and pepper. Reserve.

Peel roasted beet and use the fine side of a grater to grate 2 tablespoons (30 mL). Reserve.

to finish and serve
Preheat oven to 425°F (220°C).

Line a muffin tin with 8 paper liners. Generously spray interior of liners with spray oil. Spoon lamb mixture into liners. Gently press lamb down and flatten, level with the top of the tin.

Just before putting cupcakes into the oven, reheat potatoes by covering the bowl with aluminum foil and placing it over a pot of boiling water for 5 to 10 minutes. When potatoes are steaming hot, add grated beet. Blend thoroughly until shocking pink.

Bake cupcakes for approximately 10 minutes or until cakes are fully set yet still moist.

Use a piping bag with a star tip, or a table knife, to ice the cupcakes. If you made it to this point, nice work!

yield 8 servings **le secret** Patience and determination **uncommon goods** Vegetable oil spray, cupcake liners, muffin tin (not uncommon, but crucial), piping bag with a star tip (ideal, but not necessary) **adventure club** Top icing with a sprinkle of candied fennel seeds (available at Indian grocery stores). **level of difficulty** This is my most complex recipe. Each individual stage is infinitely doable, but collectively they require a serious commitment. **cooking times** Prep and cooking times will vary depending on how you gang up the steps. Expect to spend approximately 3 hours of active prep and 3 to 4 hours of inactive cooking time (some of which can happen simultaneously). **short-cuts** Make the Salmon Cupcakes instead (see page 188). **advance work** The lamb mixture can be prepared up to 2 days in advance, to the point that the cakes are ready to be baked. Bake and ice just before serving. Lamb mixture (or extra portions) can also be frozen, then thawed and put into the liners, and baked and iced just before serving. Mashed potatoes can be made earlier in the day, then reheated over a double boiler just before serving (add the beet after reheating). **music to cook by** Lamb, *Lamb*. A classic of vocal electronica. **liquid assets** Serve with a big, earthy red.

salmon cupcakes

This is the recipe that got me started on savory cupcakes. It was inspired by the name "fish cake," which always made me laugh when I thought of a cake made with fish. My original salmon cupcakes were bite-size and I served them as appetizers, but they quickly grew up into an adult-size entrée. Though the final look is similar to the Lamb Cupcakes, this version takes less than a quarter of the time and the effort.

3 medium russet potatoes, peeled and quartered
¼ cup (60 mL) half-and-half cream, room temperature
¼ cup (60 mL) butter, room temperature
Salt and freshly ground black pepper
2 eggs
1 pound (500 g) skinless salmon, roughly cut in ½-inch (1 cm) cubes
3 green onions, finely sliced
¼ cup (60 mL) finely chopped red bell pepper
¼ cup (60 mL) breadcrumbs or panko
¼ cup (60 mL) finely chopped fresh Italian parsley
2 tablespoons (30 mL) sour cream
Zest of 1 lemon
2 tablespoons (30 mL) freshly squeezed lemon juice
2 cloves garlic, minced
1 jalapeño chili, seeds and membranes discarded, minced
1 cup (250 mL) finely chopped fresh dill (stems discarded)

Muffin tin
8 cupcake liners
Vegetable oil spray

icing

Steam potatoes over boiling water until tender to the poke of a fork.

Use a ricer, food mill, or standard-issue fork to mash potatoes. In a medium glass or metal bowl, blend the potatoes with cream and butter, and season to taste with salt and pepper. Reserve.

cupcakes

To a food processor, add eggs, salmon, green onion, bell pepper, breadcrumbs, parsley, sour cream, lemon zest and juice, garlic, jalapeño, ½ teaspoon (2 mL) salt, and ¼ teaspoon (1 mL) freshly ground black pepper. Pulse 4 or 5 times, or until coarsely chopped and well blended. If you don't have a food processor, chop ingredients finer than indicated and blend in a bowl. Reserve. At this point the salmon mixture can be refrigerated for up to a day.

(continued . . .)

(. . . continued)

to finish and serve
Preheat oven to 400°F (200°C).

Line a muffin tin with 8 paper liners. Generously spray interior of liners with spray oil. Spoon salmon mixture into liners. Gently press salmon down and flatten, level with the top of the tin.

Just before putting salmon cupcakes in the oven, reheat potatoes by covering the bowl with aluminum foil and placing it over a pot of boiling water for 5 to 10 minutes. When potatoes are steaming hot, add dill. Blend thoroughly with a fork.

Bake cupcakes for 8 minutes, or until cakes are fully set yet still moist. Remove cakes from tin immediately so that they do not continue to cook.

Use a piping bag with a star tip, or a table knife, to ice the cupcakes.

yield 8 servings uncommon goods Vegetable oil spray, cupcake liners, muffin tin (not uncommon, but crucial), piping bag with a star tip (ideal, but not necessary) level of difficulty About the same as making cupcakes from scratch. active prep time 1 hour cooking time 15 minutes advance work The fish mixture can be prepared earlier in the day, to the point that the cakes are ready to be baked. Bake and ice just before serving. Mashed potatoes can be made earlier in the day, then reheated over a double boiler just before serving (add dill after reheating). music to cook by Arcade Fire, *Funeral.* Swirling energy from Montreal's multi-instrumental ensemble. liquid assets A Beaujolais will provide a lively match for the bright flavors of this savory cupcake.

dishwasher salmon

To promote *The Surreal Gourmet Entertains* I traveled the globe throwing spontaneous dinner parties wherever I could rustle up a kitchen and a willing audience. The hazard of having a good publicist is that guests tend to arrive with impossibly high expectations. In order to live up to their fantasies, I turned an urban legend into a practical cooking method—which earned me global notoriety and spurred on legions of Dishwasher Salmon devotees.

Poaching fish in the dishwasher is a virtually foolproof way to shock your friends, prepare a succulent meal, *and* do the dishes—all at the same time. I've poached salmon in more than 100 dishwashers on four continents, and there's never been a dull party.

My kitchen resembled a mad laboratory as I tinkered with the recipe and pushed my dishwasher well beyond the uses covered by its limited warranty. As it happens, salmon is very forgiving. Although the temperatures and durations of the cycles vary with each machine, a little more or less hot water and steam does not greatly affect the results. To heighten the drama—and prove that you have nothing up your sleeve—invite your dinner guests to crowd around the dishwasher as you load the salmon. Then, when the cycle is complete, invite them back to witness the unloading. As you open the dishwasher door, a plume of steam will rise, revealing your magically poached packets.

Here's all you need to know to set your doubts aside, put dinner in the dishwasher, and watch your multi-tasking kitchen appliance steal the show.

the instruction manual

1. Seal the salmon fillets in aluminum foil. Do not attempt to cook a whole fish (don't think it hasn't been tried).

2. Place the fish packets on the top rack.

3. Set the dishwasher to the "normal" cycle. Modern dishwashers have "economy" and "cool dry" settings, which are undesirable because they conserve heat. On the other end of the spectrum, the "pots and pans" setting tends to overcook the fish.

4. Run the salmon through the entire wash-and-dry cycle—approximately 50 minutes for most models.

5. Troubleshoot. The only time I ever had a problem was on live national TV. Five minutes before going on the air, I learned that the heating element in the on-camera dishwasher was broken. After a quick huddle with the producer, I was forced to make the most of the situation by baking the salmon in the (gasp!) oven. To avoid this pedestrian fate, ask yourself the million-dollar question: when your dishwasher last completed its cycle, were the dishes hot? As long as the answer is yes, you are ready to poach.

dishwasher salmon

1 tablespoon (15 mL) olive oil
Four 6-ounce (175 g) salmon fillets
¼ cup (60 mL) freshly squeezed lemon juice
Salt and freshly ground black pepper
1 lemon, sliced
4 sprigs fresh dill

Heavy-duty aluminum foil

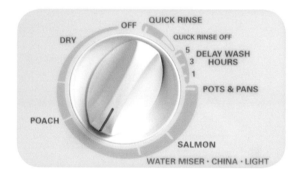

Cut two 14-inch (35 cm) square sheets of aluminum foil.

Grease the shiny side of the foil with the oil. Place 2 fillets side by side on each square and fold up the outer edges.

Drizzle 1 tablespoon (15 mL) of lemon juice over each fillet. Season with salt and pepper. Top with a lemon slice and a sprig of dill.

Fold and pinch aluminum foil extra tightly to create a watertight seal around each pair of fillets. Make sure the packets are airtight by pressing down gently on each one with your hand. If any air escapes, rewrap.

Place the foil packets on the top rack of the dishwasher. Run the dishwasher for the entire "normal" cycle.

When cycle is complete, take out salmon, discard foil, and place one fillet on each plate. (Note: Don't be concerned about the opaque white beads that may appear on the fillets. They are simply a redistribution of the salmon's natural fats.) If you have made the optional Piquant Dill Sauce, spoon a generous serving overtop fillets.

optional piquant dill sauce

1 tablespoon (15 mL) butter
1 leek, white and pale green section only, diced
1 shallot, minced
1 jalapeño chili, seeds and membranes discarded, diced
2 cloves garlic, minced
1 cup (250 mL) chicken stock
1½ cups (375 mL) lightly packed fresh dill (stems discarded)
2 tablespoons (30 mL) freshly squeezed lemon juice
Salt and freshly ground black pepper
3 tablespoons (45 mL) sour cream

In a sauté pan over medium heat, melt butter.

Add leek, shallot, jalapeño, and garlic, and sauté for approximately 5 minutes, or until the leeks and shallots are translucent—but not brown.

Add the stock. Simmer, uncovered, for 15 minutes. Adjust heat as required to maintain simmer and reduce liquid by half. Remove from heat and let cool.

Transfer liquid to a blender or food processor and add dill and lemon juice. Purée until smooth. Season to taste with salt and pepper. Reserve.

To serve, rewarm over low heat and stir in the sour cream at the last minute.

yield 4 servings of salmon and approximately 1 cup (250 mL) dill sauce **le secret** Make sure other items in the dishwasher, such as silverware, are securely stowed so that they do not fly around and pierce the foil packets. **level of difficulty** As easy as loading the dishwasher. **active prep time** 25 minutes **inactive cooking time** 60 minutes **shortcuts** Skip the sauce. **advance work** Salmon packets can be wrapped earlier in the day. **oven method** Don't have a dishwasher? Bake foil-wrapped packets in a preheated 400°F (200°C) oven for 12 minutes. **music to poach by** Sigur Rós, *Ágætis byrjun*. The second album from the atmospheric Icelandic band. If you like the album, you must check out the stunning DVD *Heima*, which chronicles their tour of churches, schools, and other out-of-the-way venues in their homeland. **liquid assets** Australian Chardonnay. A little thunder from down under.

meatloaf surprise

I created this recipe for a children's birthday party–themed episode of *Surreal Gourmet*. When the kids first saw the cake, they were ecstatic and assumed that in TV land everyone gets to eat their dessert first. Then they took their first bites and, contrary to what ended up in the final cut, there were more than a few tears. Eventually, even the most disappointed kids warmed up to the idea. I rewarded them with a real chocolate cake that I presented to look like a hamburger. I doubt that any of those kids will ever trust me again.

4 cups (1 L) stale bread, cut in ½-inch (1 cm) pieces
3½ cups (875 mL) milk, divided
2 tablespoons (30 mL) olive oil
1 onion, diced
4 pounds (1.8 kg) ground chuck (hamburger)
3 eggs
3 cups (750 mL) finely chopped fresh Italian parsley (stems discarded), divided
2 tablespoons (30 mL) fresh thyme (stems discarded)
1 teaspoon (5 mL) salt
½ teaspoon (2 mL) pepper
½ teaspoon (2 mL) freshly grated nutmeg
½ cup (125 mL) ketchup
8 russet potatoes, peeled and cut in 1-inch (2.5 cm) pieces
¼ cup (60 mL) butter, plus more for greasing pans
1 head broccoli, cut in florets
2 carrots, peeled and sliced in ⅛-inch-thick (3 mm) slices
1 pint cherry tomatoes

cakes

Preheat oven to 400°F (200°C).

Place bread in a bowl. Add 2 cups (500 mL) milk and toss with bread. Reserve.

In a sauté pan over medium-high heat, add 2 tablespoons (30 mL) oil and sauté onion for approximately 4 minutes, or until it becomes translucent. Reserve.

In a large bowl, use your hands to mix the chuck, eggs, 1 cup (250 mL) parsley, thyme, salt, pepper, nutmeg, soaked bread, onions, and ketchup.

Divide meatloaf mixture into two equal amounts and spoon into 2 greased 10-inch (25 cm) round baking pans. Smooth tops so that they are flat. Bake for 1¼ hours. Reserve.

(continued . . .)

(. . . continued)

icing

While meatloaf is cooking, steam or boil potatoes until tender to the poke of a fork. Use a ricer, food mill, or standard-issue fork to mash potatoes. Slowly add 1 cup (250 mL) milk and butter. Blend until smooth. Cover and reserve.

In a blender, purée remaining parsley and ½ cup (125 mL) milk. Reserve.

Divide mashed potatoes into a 4-cup (1 L) batch and a 2-cup (500 mL) batch. Save whatever is left over for a rainy day. Reserve the 2-cup (500 mL) batch.

In a large bowl, thoroughly blend the puréed parsley into the 4-cup (1 L) batch of mashed potatoes. Cover and reserve.

After the meatloaf has finished baking, steam broccoli and carrots in a vegetable steamer for approximately 4 minutes, or until tender. Transfer to an ice bath. Once cool, pat dry with a paper towel. Reserve.

to finish and serve

Remove meatloaves from pans. Place the first meatloaf on a cake stand, or a regular plate. Spread the top with half of the plain (white) mashed potatoes. Place second meatloaf on top, and ice the whole "cake" with the green mashed potatoes just as you would ice a birthday cake.

Place the remaining cup (250 mL) of plain mashed potatoes in a piping bag with a star tip, or a resealable plastic bag with one corner snipped. Pipe out little potato crowns around the parameter of the top of the cake, leaving a 2-inch (5 cm) space in between each one. Top with cherry tomatoes. Decorate with broccoli, carrots, and candles, if desired.

yield Serves 8 unhappy kids! **uncommon goods** 2 matching 10-inch (25 cm) round baking pans, piping bag with a star tip (ideal, but not necessary) **level of difficulty** Like baking a layer cake. **active prep/cooking time** 90 minutes **inactive cooking time** 75 minutes **variation on a theme** For pink icing, replace parsley purée with ¼ cup (60 mL) of grated, roasted beet. **advance work** The meatloaf mixture can be prepared earlier in the day, to the point that the cakes are to be baked. Bake and ice just before serving. Mashed potatoes can be made earlier in the day, then reheated over a double boiler just before serving (add any coloring ingredients after reheating). **music to cook by** *The Royal Philharmonic Orchestra Plays the Music of Meatloaf.* All the fun of original Meatloaf but now with more strings. (There are no vocals, so you're free to sing along.) **liquid assets** Milk

fleur de poulet

This Fleur de Poulet is one of the entrées I dreamed up for my Paris cooking debut. In the spring of 2005, I was hired by Toyota to helm a disposable restaurant in Paris for a week. Sparing no expense, they parachuted a professional kitchen into a huge photo studio and created seating for 50 on the level below. It was all part of a viral campaign for the launch of their sporty little Aygo. For five days, along with my crack team of French-trained sous chefs, I served up a set menu of surreal lunches and dinners to the Parisian media and glitterati. After the last meal was served, the ephemeral restaurant disappeared overnight without so much as a trace of breadcrumbs. Much to my amazement, it all came off without a hitch. In retrospect, I see it as my culinary coming of age.

2 symmetrical yams or sweet potatoes
4 large boneless, skinless chicken breasts
Salt and freshly ground black pepper
2 cups (500 mL) pineapple juice
2 tablespoons (30 mL) freshly squeezed lime juice
1 tablespoon (15 mL) olive oil
4 thick asparagus spears, trimmed and peeled at the bottom
12 fresh mint leaves
2 tablespoons (30 mL) toasted sunflower seeds

To bake yams, set toaster oven to 425°F (220°C) and bake whole for 1 hour, or until small sugar beads begin to form on skins. Reserve. If you don't have a toaster oven, bake in advance in oven.

To bake chicken, preheat oven to 250°F (120°C) (this is not a typo!).

Remove chicken tenders. Save for a rainy day.

Season chicken with salt and pepper. Set chicken in a nonreactive baking dish that is just large enough to accommodate it, and add pineapple and lime juices. Seal tightly with aluminum foil.

Bake chicken for approximately 60 to 75 minutes, or until cooked throughout and no longer pink in the middle. Remove 1 cup (250 mL) of marinade, then re-cover and let chicken rest in the remaining juices.

In a small pan over high heat, reduce the cup of marinade by about half, until it is a thick glaze. Reserve.

In a sauté pan over medium-high heat, add olive oil. Add asparagus and a pinch of salt. Turn a quarter rotation every minute or so until asparagus begins to brown on all sides. Reserve.

(continued . . .)

(. . . continued)

to finish and serve

Slice chicken breasts crosswise into ¼-inch-thick (6 mm) slices.

Carefully peel skin off yams and then cut into ½-inch-thick (1 cm) slices.

Assemble flowers on the plate by using yams as the center, 5 or 6 chicken slices as the petals, asparagus as the stem and mint leaves as the . . . yes, leaves. Then brush chicken with the glaze and top yam with sunflower seeds.

yield 4 servings **le secret** If you trust the slow cooking method, it will deliver juicy, succulent chicken. **level of difficulty** As easy as poaching an egg. **active prep time** 40 minutes **inactive cooking time** 75 minutes **shortcuts** Skip the fancy presentation. **advance work** Chicken can be baked earlier in the day. Keep whole in marinade, then reheat just before serving. Alternatively, the whole dish can be prepared in advance and served at room temperature for a summer dinner. Slice chicken just before serving. **multiplicity** Additional pieces of chicken will require approximately half the amount of marinade. **music to cook by** Various artists, *Amélie* soundtrack. The sound of Paris, in all of its romantic glory. **liquid assets** Viognier, which is often described as pineappley (you can taste it if you try hard enough!), will play well off the marinade.

turkey parfait

According to the Surreal Gourmet Institute of Culinary Research, the average Thanksgiving feast requires two months of negotiating, three weeks of planning, no less than 14 shopping trips, 23½ hours of prep time, 5 hours of cooking, and 12 hours of baking. At mealtime, the first serving is inhaled in a matter of minutes, and seconds are scarfed down in . . . well . . . seconds. Desserts dissolve into thin air. Then everybody falls into a tryptamine-induced coma and it's all over but for the cleanup.

Once so much energy has been put into preparing a festive bird and the usual constellation of traditional side dishes that accompany it, it's only fair that you should get more out of your leftovers than just a turkey sandwich. Feel free to substitute whatever leftovers you have for the ones I have suggested.

1 cup (250 mL) leftover turkey, torn or cut in small pieces
⅔ cup (160 mL) leftover mashed potatoes
⅔ cup (160 mL) leftover squash
⅔ cup (160 mL) leftover greens
2 leftover roasted Brussels sprouts
½ cup (125 mL) cranberry sauce

2 parfait glasses or similar facsimiles

Reheat turkey, potatoes, squash, greens, and Brussels sprouts in an oven or microwave.

To assemble the parfait, use a spoon to layer the turkey, squash, greens, and cranberry sauce in individual parfait glasses. Finish with an ice-cream scoop of mashed potatoes, and top with a roasted Brussels sprout.

yield 2 servings **uncommon goods** 2 parfait glasses **level of difficulty** As easy as assembling an ice-cream parfait. **active prep time** 10 minutes **shortcuts** If you have a microwave oven, assemble the parfait whole to begin with, then microwave it all at once. **advance work** It's all already been done! **music to cook by** Arlo Guthrie, *Alice's Restaurant*. Pray that your turkey dinner doesn't suffer the same fate. **liquid assets** Any wine left over from the previous night's turkey dinner

shrimp on the barbie

Whether these shrimp are cooked on the stove or an outdoor grill, they disappear faster than Barbie can change her profession.

shrimp
1 pound (500 g) raw 21/25 count shrimp, peeled and deveined (tails may be left on)
2 tablespoons (30 mL) dried oregano
1 tablespoon (15 mL) dried thyme
1 teaspoon (5 mL) lemon pepper seasoning
¼–½ teaspoon (1–2 mL) ground dried chipotle or a pinch of cayenne pepper
½ teaspoon (2 mL) salt
½ teaspoon (2 mL) freshly ground black pepper
2 tablespoons (30 mL) olive oil

PAN VERSION
In a medium bowl, mix all dry seasonings. Add shrimp and toss thoroughly. In a large sauté pan over high heat, add oil. When oil is hot, add as many shrimp as pan will accommodate without overlapping. Cook for approximately 1 minute per side, or until no longer translucent.

GRILL VERSION
Preheat grill to high direct heat (see page 247). In a medium bowl, mix all dry seasonings.

Pour oil into a large bowl. Add shrimp and toss. Sprinkle seasonings overtop and toss to coat. Grill for 1 minute per side, or until shrimp are no longer translucent.

cilantro dipping sauce
1 cup (250 mL) lightly packed fresh cilantro leaves (stems discarded)
3 tablespoons (45 mL) freshly squeezed lime juice
½ cup (125 mL) sour cream

Blend cilantro and lime juice in a blender or a small food processor until liquefied. Spoon sour cream into a small bowl and slowly stir in liquid. Reserve in refrigerator. Serve with shrimp.

yield Serves 6 as an appetizer with ¾ cup (185 mL) of dipping sauce uncommon goods Barbie doll alarming advice Unhook your smoke alarm before pan-searing the shrimp (but don't forget to reconnect it). level of difficulty As easy as playing with dolls. active prep time 20 minutes cooking time 5 minutes shortcuts Skip the cilantro bit for the dipping sauce and just add a squeeze of lime to the sour cream. advance work Dry rub can be made ahead and stored in a sealed jar. Make extra—it lasts almost indefinitely. multiplicity Dipping sauce will accommodate an extra batch of shrimp music to cook by David Bowie, *The Rise and Fall of Ziggy Stardust and the Spiders from Mars.* A glam manifesto. liquid assets A Victoria Bitter (VB) or Foster's Lager—the wizards of Oz

frosty the mashed-potato snowman

My fondest winter memories revolve around my childhood house on Apple Hill Road in Baie-d'Urfé, a sleepy suburban enclave on the West Island of Montreal. I remember playing hockey on the skating rink my dad made in our backyard, and tunneling through the mountainous snowbanks in the front yard that were formed in the wake of the city's plows. At least they seemed mountainous at the time.

Until recently I blamed global warming for the diminishing size of the snowbanks I see kids playing in. Then it struck me that, in addition to changes caused by the current climate crisis, my perspective has changed—by about three feet.

When I was asked to create a recipe for a Food Network Christmas special, I combined my love of playing in the snow with my love of playing with my food. The result was a mashed-potato side dish infused with heartwarming, mouth-melting, freshly grated horseradish, and accessorized to look like a miniature snowman. These spud sculptures are fun to decorate, fun to eat (where should you start?), cheerfully nondenominational, and equally as appreciated by kids as by the kid that still dwells within us all.

4 medium-large russet potatoes, peeled and cut in eighths
¼ cup (60 mL) butter
¼ cup (60 mL) half-and-half cream
2 tablespoons (30 mL) finely grated fresh horseradish or 1 tablespoon (15 mL) prepared
   horseradish (optional, and not so appreciated by fussy-eater kids like I used to be)
Salt and white pepper
8 rosemary sprigs
4 small carrots
8 large black olives (often sold as "colossal")
8 whole cloves
24 pink peppercorns
12 black peppercorns
4 strips of rind from 1 lemon

Three ice-cream scoops, approximately 1¼, 2, and 2¼ inches (3 cm, 5 cm, and 5.5 cm)
   in diameter

Steam potatoes until they are tender to the poke of a fork (about 20 minutes).

Use a ricer, food mill, or fork to mash potatoes. Add butter, cream, horseradish (if using), and salt and pepper. Mix until smooth. Adjust to taste with salt, pepper, and additional horseradish. Reserve.

(continued . . .)

(. . . continued)

to finish and serve

Trim rosemary, and cut carrots, olives, and lemon as per photo.

Reheat potatoes by covering the bowl with aluminum foil and placing it over a pot of boiling water for 5 to 10 minutes, or until steaming hot.

Use ice-cream scoops to form your snowmen. Dress 'em, serve 'em, and eat 'em.

yield 4 snowmen uncommon goods 3 ice-cream scoops, approximately 1¼, 2, and 2¼ inches (3 cm, 5 cm, and 5.5 cm) in diameter; fresh horseradish (available in specialty grocery stores) level of difficulty The only difficult part is assembling the snowmen quickly just before serving. active prep time 1½ hours inactive cooking time 20 minutes shortcuts This one is all or nothing. advance work Mashed potatoes can be prepared earlier in the day, then reheated over a double boiler just before serving. Carrot noses, rosemary arms, lemon-rind scarves, and olive hats can be sculpted earlier in the day. music to cook by Rudolph, Frosty & Friends' Favorite Christmas Songs. All the Xmas faves from the 70s TV specials make for a warm and fuzzy trip down holiday memory lane.

flowerpot salad

Many of my signature presentations evolve as I circle the globe preparing surreal meals in far-flung—and often far-out—places. Some of the new twists are by design, some rise from the ashes of disasters, and some are the culinary consequence of dialogues that were lost in translation. But in every case, they are the results of collaborating with talented chefs who rise to the occasion of presenting my trompe l'oeil dishes. I am indebted to the chefs at the InterContinental hotel in Singapore, whose resourcefulness elevated the presentation of this salad I served for the World Gourmet Summit.

6 ounces (175 g) mixed baby greens (ideally containing baby herbs)
3 tablespoons (45 mL) crushed toasted hazelnuts
¼ cup (60 mL) (about 1½ ounces/45 g) shaved Parmigiano Reggianno
1 cup (250 mL) Maple-Dijon Dressing recipe (that's 4 times the recipe on page 94—not all of the dressing is consumed, but it will last for weeks in your fridge) or your favorite vinaigrette
Salt and freshly ground black pepper
1 pint edible flowers such as nasturtiums and pansies

4 small plastic flowerpots
1 plastic watering can (optional)

In a large bowl, add greens, hazelnuts, Parmigiano, and approximately 2 tablespoons (30 mL) dressing, or just enough to very lightly dress the greens. Gently toss. Season to taste with salt and pepper. Fill pot with salad, then top with flowers.

Serve with a food-safe watering can containing extra dressing. At the table, drizzle a small bit of dressing overtop each pot.

yield 4 salad servings uncommon goods Edible flowers, plastic flowerpots (available at gardening shops and some hardware stores), plastic watering can level of difficulty Like making a salad for arts-and-crafts class. active prep time 45 minutes shortcuts Skip the flowerpot. advance work Dressing can be made up to a couple of days in advance. multiplicity Dressing will accommodate up to 16 servings. music to cook by Various artists, *Summer of Love: The Hits of 1967*. Be sure to wear some flowers in your hair.

cereal killer soup

I made this soup in a breakfast-for-dinner episode of *The Surreal Gourmet*. My guests were a group of Toronto taxi drivers who worked the all-night shift and were accustomed to eating dinner after the sun rose. They came from all walks of life and all corners of the globe—and dispensed their cab-driver wisdom liberally.

Lucky for them, they weren't really getting cold cereal for supper. And lucky for me, I got to hang out in my Toastermobile with some very wise men.

4 tablespoons (60 mL) butter, divided
1 tablespoon (15 mL) Indian spice blend (e.g. garam masala)
1 cup (250 mL) Cheerios
1 medium onion, roughly chopped
1 leek, white and pale green section only, diced
1 head cauliflower, trimmed and roughly chopped
6 cups (1.5 L) chicken or vegetable broth, divided
Salt and white pepper to taste
¼ teaspoon (1 mL) freshly grated nutmeg (ideally)
1 tablespoon (15 mL) freshly squeezed lemon juice
¼–½ cup (60–125 mL) half-and-half cream (optional)

Preheat oven to 350°F (180°C).

In a sauté pan over medium heat, melt 2 tablespoons (30 mL) butter and add spice blend. Add Cheerios and toss thoroughly. Transfer spiced Cheerios to a sheet pan and bake for 10 minutes, or until crispy. Reserve.

In a medium pot over medium heat, add 2 tablespoons (30 mL) butter and sauté onion and leek for about 4 minutes, or until translucent. Add cauliflower and 5 cups (1.25 L) of broth. Bring to a boil. Reduce heat and let simmer for approximately 20 minutes, or until cauliflower is completely soft.

Purée contents of pot in a blender until smooth. If necessary, thin with remaining broth until soup is your desired consistency. For extra-smooth soup, run the purée through a fine strainer. Discard any solids. Season with salt, white pepper, and nutmeg. Finish with lemon juice.

To serve, reheat to a gentle simmer. If you choose to increase the richness quotient, add approximately 2 tablespoons (30 mL) of cream per serving while reheating. Pour soup into a cereal-style bowl and sprinkle generously with the spiced Cheerios.

yield 6 servings **uncommon goods** Chicken or vegetable broth. Broth is lighter in color than stock and will help contribute to a whiter soup. It can be found in most grocery stores, but is easily confused with stock. **level of difficulty** Easy **active prep time** 45 minutes **cooking time** 20 minutes **advance work** Can be made up to 2 days in advance. **music to cook by** Henry Mancini, *Breakfast at Tiffany's: Music From the Motion Picture Score*. Too bad Audrey is no longer accepting breakfast invitations.

faux fries

Who wouldn't love french fries for dessert?

faux fries

1 loaf of pound cake (store-bought, such as Entenmann's)

1 fast-food french-fry container (ask politely and you shall receive)

Preheat oven to 350°F (180°C).

Trim the dome off the top of the loaf and a thin layer of crust off all remaining sides of the loaf. Then cut about 2 inches (5 cm) off one end of the loaf so that the remaining block is approximately 4 × 3 × 6 inches (10 cm × 8 cm × 15 cm). Cut remaining loaf lengthwise into ¼-inch (6 mm) slices. Set slices flat on their sides and cut lengthwise again into ¼-inch (6 mm) strips.

Arrange strips on a cookie sheet and bake for approximately 10 minutes, or until browned on top and bottom. Turn strips a quarter rotation and bake for approximately 4 more minutes, or until remaining 2 sides are browned. Let cool, then arrange in fries container.

raspberry ketchup

6 ounces (175 g) frozen raspberries, thawed, or 1 cup (250 mL) of fresh raspberries
2 tablespoons (30 mL) confectioner's (icing) sugar

1 empty ketchup bottle or plastic squeeze bottle

If you are using frozen berries, drain off the excess juice. Purée raspberries in a blender or food processor. Add the sugar, 1 teaspoon (5 mL) at a time, to taste—until the tartness is gone.

Place the raspberry purée in a strainer over a bowl. Use a rubber spatula or the back of a spoon to force the purée through the strainer. Discard the seeds and transfer the purée to the ketchup bottle. Serve alongside the "fries."

yield 4 dessert servings or 8 tastes le secret Keep a watchful eye on the fries as they bake. uncommon goods 1 fast-food french-fry container; 1 empty ketchup bottle or plastic squeeze bottle; 1 loaf of pound cake (a common grocery item that is not always available when you need it) level of difficulty Easier than making real french fries. active prep time 20 minutes cooking time 15 minutes shortcuts Skip the raspberry ketchup, or buy raspberry sauce (sometimes sold as coulis). advance work Fries can be made up to a day in advance and stored in an airtight container. Ketchup can be made up to 2 days in advance. multiplicity One batch of ketchup will usually last for up to 4 containers of fries. music to cook by Autour de Lucie, *Faux mouvement*. Seductive French indie-pop.

jell-o slicers

Now you can do Jell-O shooters and maintain your dignity.

2 oranges
1 regular-size package orange-flavored Jell-O
½ cup (125 mL) vanilla vodka (or your favorite orange-complementing flavor)

Slice the oranges in half. Using a regular dinner spoon, scoop out all the flesh and divider pith. Reserve the shells.

In a medium bowl, add the Jell-O and ½ cup (125 mL) of boiling water. When the Jell-O has dissolved, add the vodka. Pour the liquid Jell-O into the orange halves. Refrigerate for approximately 4 hours, or until firm. To serve, slice each half into 3 wedges. REMEMBER, YOU ARE SERVING SOLID BOOZE.

yield 12 hangovers **level of difficulty** You're basically making Jell-O. **active prep time** 20 minutes **inactive prep time** 4 hours **shortcuts** Squeeze the oranges (plus a few extras), add vodka, and serve over ice. **advance work** Can be made up to a few days in advance. **variations on a theme** Apply the same concept to lemons or limes. **music to cook by** XTC, *Oranges & Lemons*

chocolate wontons

Think about how much you love crispy, crunchy Chinese or Vietnamese spring rolls. Now imagine how good they would taste if you replaced the bamboo shoots, water chestnuts, green onions, and so on with melted milk chocolate, gooey caramel, crunchy peanut butter, and slices of ripe banana. It's a decadent combination that won't leave you hungry in an hour.

Eight 3½-inch (9 cm) square wonton wrappers
¼ cup (60 mL) peanut butter (smooth or crunchy—your choice!)
1 banana, peeled and sliced in ¼-inch-thick (6 mm) slices
8 Rolo or Caramilk bar segments
Peanut oil (for deep frying)
Confectioner's/icing sugar, for dusting (optional)

Place a small bowl of warm water beside wonton wrappers. Put a single wonton wrapper on a clean, dry surface in front of you. Schmear 1 teaspoon (5 mL) of peanut butter onto the center. Press down a banana slice on top of peanut butter and top with chocolate. Dip your finger in water and trace a circle on the wonton wrapper around the stack of ingredients (water is the glue of wonton wrappers). Pinch and seal wrapper around the ingredients. Be sure that seams are tightly sealed to keep frying oil from seeping in.

Before frying, see Fear of Frying (page 246).

Pour oil into a small, tall pot until it is 3 inches (8 cm) deep. Heat oil until it reaches 350°F (177°C).

When oil is ready, fry 4 wontons at a time for approximately 1 minute, or until wonton wrappers are golden brown. Remove and place on a paper towel to absorb excess oil. Dust with sugar (if desired). Let cool for 1 minute before serving.

building a better chopstick

yield 8 dessert wontons **uncommon goods** Wonton wrappers (available in Asian groceries and in the refrigerated or frozen section of most grocery stores), oil thermometer. If you don't have an oil thermometer, drop a piece of wonton wrapper into the oil around the time you think the oil is ready. It's at the right temperature if the wrapper gets crispy in 5 to 8 seconds. **level of difficulty** Wonton wrapping takes a bit of practice, but each wrapper costs about 3 cents so mistakes are cheap. **active prep time** 15 minutes **cooking time** 5 minutes **advance work** Wontons can be wrapped earlier in the day. Cover with a damp dishtowel and refrigerate. Do not let the wontons touch. To minimize stickage, dust the surface of the storage plate and the wontons themselves with cornstarch. **multiplicity** Additional wontons do not require extra frying oil. **music to cook by** Carolina Chocolate Drops, *Genuine Negro Jig*. Old-time string band music gets a new lease on life.

dog bones

Generous amounts of freshly grated ginger and white pepper give these gingerbread cookies for real people some real bite.

2 cups (500 mL) granulated sugar
1 cup (250 mL) salted butter, room temperature
⅔ cup (160 mL) molasses
2 eggs
3 tablespoons (45 mL) peeled and finely grated fresh ginger
½ tablespoon (7.5 mL) apple cider vinegar (needed to react with the baking soda)
6 cups (1.5 L) all-purpose flour (plus extra to dust the rolling surface)
1 tablespoon (15 mL) white pepper
1 tablespoon (15 mL) ground cinnamon
½ teaspoon (2 mL) ground cloves
1½ teaspoons (7.5 mL) baking soda

Preheat oven to 325°F (160°C).

In a large bowl, combine sugar, butter, molasses, eggs, ginger, and vinegar.

In a second large bowl, combine flour, pepper, cinnamon, cloves, and baking soda. Blend the contents of bowl #2 into bowl #1.

Wrap dough in plastic wrap and refrigerate for 1 hour (this allows the dough to harden so that it can be rolled out).

Sprinkle rolling surface with flour. Roll out dough to a ⅜-inch (9 mm) thickness.

Use a 3-inch (8 cm) bone-shaped cookie cutter to stamp out cookies. After cutting the first batch, knead the trimmings together and reroll.

Bake on a baking sheet for 12 to 15 minutes, or until they begin to brown.

yield 24 biscuits **uncommon goods** Empty dog-biscuit box, dog bone–shaped cookie cutter **level of difficulty** As easy as baking cookies. **active prep time** 30 minutes **inactive prep time** 1 hour **cooking time** 15 minutes **shortcuts** Skip the doggie theme. **advance work** Dough or fully baked cookies can be made days in advance. **music to cook by** George Thorogood & the Destroyers, *Bad to the Bone*. B-b-bluesy slide guitar rock. **liquid assets** Baileys Irish Cream on the rocks is the milk that will mellow the spiciness of these cookies.

existential eggs

This edible trompe l'oeil looks like a soft-boiled egg, and runs like a soft-boiled egg, but one spoonful will reveal that the tasty yolk is on your guests. Since I created the dessert for *Surreal Gourmet Bites*, it has become my favorite finale for my Surreal Meal gigs. In collaboration with some of the chefs I have worked with at these dinners, I have refined the original recipe and presentation. I now make the yolk from passion fruit instead of the original mango because I find that the acidity of the passion fruit tempers the sweetness of the white chocolate. And by filling it from the cut end of the eggshell, you will be able to flip it and conceal the cut end in an eggcup—which creates the illusion that the egg has not been tampered with. This allows you to cut the top off the eggshell in front of your perplexed guests, adding a deliciously Dalí-esque twist to the evening.

12 eggs, ideally brown (plus extras for safety)

¾ teaspoon (4 mL) unflavored gelatin

12 ounces (375 g) white baker's chocolate, chopped in teeny-weeny bits, divided

1½ cups (375 mL) cold heavy cream, divided

1 teaspoon (5 mL) vanilla extract

18 passion fruits; or 1½ cups (375 mL) frozen pure passion fruit purée; or 3 ripe, fragrant
    mangoes, peeled, seeded, and puréed

1 egg carton (for use in assembling the eggs)

1 eggcup per guest

Using a sharp knife, carefully chop off the fatter bottom side of the eggs, in the same manner as you would cut the top off a soft-boiled egg. Remove the eggs from the shells and reserve them in a tightly sealed jar for your next breakfast (they will last a couple of days). Run the eggshells under very hot water (be careful) to clean out any egg-white residue. Use your finger to roll away the thin membrane that covers the interior of the shell. Reserve shells in egg carton.

In a small bowl, add 3 tablespoons (45 mL) of cold water. Sprinkle gelatin overtop and let stand for 5 minutes. Reserve.

In a large bowl, add 8 ounces (250 g) chocolate.

In a small pot, bring ½ cup (125 mL) of cream to a boil. Add dissolved gelatin and vanilla, and stir for 30 seconds.

Pour cream over chocolate and whisk until smooth.

Refrigerate for 30 minutes, or until chocolate thickens but still falls off a spoon.

(continued . . .)

(. . . continued)

In a stand mixer or a large bowl, whip remaining 1 cup (250 mL) of cream until it forms stiff peaks.

Using a rubber spatula, gently but thoroughly fold whipped cream into chocolate mixture. Return to refrigerator for 2 hours, or until it has set.

To make passion fruit purée, scoop out 12 passion fruits, then press fruit through a strainer to remove the seeds. Transfer juice to a plastic container or pan that is small enough to allow juice to be ½ inch (1 cm) deep. Freeze. When juice is frozen solid, cut into ½-inch (1 cm) cubes. Reserve in freezer.

assembly

Before starting, refer to the series of how-to diagrams on page 255. Transfer white chocolate mousse (that's what it is now) to a pastry bag, or a large resealable plastic bag with its corner clipped. Set eggshells in the carton, cut side up. Fill one-third of each eggshell with mousse. Set a passion fruit yolk in the center of each shell and push it down slightly into mousse. Pipe more mousse over yolk, being careful not to leave any air pockets, and fill egg to ¼-inch (6 mm) below the lip of the shell. Reserve in refrigerator.

Melt remaining white chocolate over a double boiler. Spoon 1 tablespoon (15 mL) over the open end of each egg to plug it up. Return to refrigerator for a minimum of 1 hour, until the chocolate plug hardens and the yolks thaw (so that they run when cut into).

Serve in eggcups, pointy side up (i.e. plugged side on the bottom, hidden by the cup). Slice off the top of the shell in front of your guests.

yield 12 servings. Once you are going to all this trouble, there is no sense in only making a few. (See advance work below for what to do with extras.) **uncommon goods** Gelatin, white baker's chocolate, passion fruits or frozen passion fruit purée, eggcups **level of difficulty** Making this recipe is like learning an elaborate card trick. It seems tricky to pull off at the outset, but when decoded it's actually quite simple. **active prep time** 1½ hours **inactive prep time** 4 hours **advance work** Eggs can be made up to 3 days in advance. Refrigerate in an egg carton wrapped with plastic wrap. Extra eggs will last in the freezer for a month. If freezing, transfer to the fridge 4 hours before serving. **music to cook by** Shrift, *Lost in a Moment*. Lovely, ambient pop with global influences, featuring the hypnotic voice of Nina Miranda. **liquid assets** Moscato d'Asti is a semisweet Italian sparkling wine that is just light and fruity enough to support the overt sweetness of the white chocolate mousse.

the perfect martini

I always thought gin martinis were for James Bond wannabes and members of our parents' generation. Then I tasted Victoria Gin. After one sip I was infatuated. After the second I fell in love. And after the third, I bought part of the company. Such is the story of my shotgun romance with Victoria Spirits, the family-operated boutique gin distiller from Vancouver Island. Whether you use this distinctively handcrafted, wood-fired gin or another small-batch artisanal gin, here's the ideal way to appreciate its aromatic botanicals.

12 ice cubes
3 ounces (90 mL) Victoria Gin
1 contemplation of vermouth
2 lemon twists

2 martini glasses
1 martini shaker or teapot

Drop 2 ice cubes and a splash of water into each martini glass. Add remaining cubes to shaker.

Add gin to shaker, being careful not to overpour by more than an ounce or two.

Contemplate the loneliness of vermouth, pause, and continue on to the next step.

Shake or stir until the sharp edges of the ice cubes melt into submission.

Empty out ice and water from the glasses.

Gently caress the entire rim of each glass with the exterior skin side of a lemon twist, then drop twist into glass.

Strain invigorated gin into the chilled-out glasses.

Make eye contact with your partner in crime, clink glasses, and bask in the glow of your sublime good fortune.

Repeat as necessary.

stop and smell the rosés

adventures in wine

I always appreciated wine, but until my mid-30s, I was frustrated and intimidated by the secret language and rituals of the swirling, gurgling, nosing, wine-drinking cognoscenti. Deep down, it bugged me that they seemed to know so much more than I did. Part of me was also suspicious that all the fuss was a classic case of "the emperor's new clothes." In an attempt to tutor myself, I invested in a couple of mixed cases of wine and dove in—corkscrew first. I was sucked in, and quickly learned that once you trust your instincts, the great mysteries slowly unmask themselves—regardless of where you are on the wine ladder. In fact, after you get familiar with some of the terminology, you will likely discover that your intuitions were correct all along—you just didn't have the vocabulary to express what you were experiencing. As a bonus, once you demonstrate an interest in wine, those same discriminating winos you once ridiculed will come out of the woodwork to share their knowledge (and wine) with you. I should know. I have turned into one of those people.

wine 1.0

THE COMPLEX WORLD OF WINE can be very intimidating. But with a little self-less dedication and this brief primer, you can quickly gain the confidence to trust your instincts and build a relationship with the grape, which will only get better over time—just like a fine wine.

look for your true love

Wine is a very personal matter. There is no reason that you should be attracted to what everybody else likes—even if the "experts" gush about it. To empower yourself to find the wines that please your palate, start by paying attention to every glass you drink. Scribble notes, snap a photo of the label on your phone, and steal a taste from everybody's glass the moment they turn their back. Eventually, you will notice that the wines you prefer share certain characteristics. In all likelihood, the common denominator will be the varietal (type of grape) that the wine is made from. Once you have discovered the varietal(s) you like, you have arrived at the real beginning of your wine enlightenment. From that point, you can go on to compare and determine for yourself the specific regions and producers within that genre—and within your budget—that please you the most. And don't be surprised if, over time, your tastes evolve. I was lured into the wine world by uncomplicated, instantly gratifying, jammy Beaujolais. But now I seek out dusty, earthy, skanky wines that I would literally have spit out in my early days.

be blind

It is not uncommon for someone to melt over a wine that seems uninspiring to you—and vice versa. Don't let a difference in opinion intimidate you, but do let it motivate you to give a wine a second chance. In order to ensure a fair trial under any set of circumstances, use your best efforts to block out the distractions in the room and focus your senses on what is in the glass. Sometimes the greatest distractions in judging a wine are its price, label, and reputation. A good way to block out these influences is to conduct your own blind tasting. All it takes are a few paper bags and a homemade scorecard. These tastings are fun to do with friends and inevitably produce results that are surprising, if not downright scandalous.

don't swallow

Different parts of your tongue are sensitive to different tastes. To fully appreciate the virtues of a wine, don't swallow it immediately—roll it all around your tongue and savor the full range of its characteristics. With your first sip, try to suck air into your mouth over the wine. In addition to making a ridiculous gurgling sound, this will cause the flavors to explode on your tongue and the back of your mouth, giving you an instant impression of the wine (for those of you with pierced tongues, try not to dribble). After swallowing, count how long the flavors linger in your mouth. As a rule of thumb, the longer the "finish," the better the wine. Your average swill tends to disappear in seconds, while fine wines can linger in your mouth for more than a minute.

find the right partner

Wine, like sex, can be enjoyed alone, but is infinitely more pleasurable when accompanied by the right partner. Some fine wines, such as very dry Bordeaux, actually suffer when consumed without food because they need protein to counterbalance their tannins (one of the sources of their dryness). Once you have led yourself to wines you like, the next challenge is pairing them. Forget the antiquated rules of food-and-wine pairing. Just think in broad strokes and let common sense guide you to wines that enhance the flavors of specific dishes. Accompany highly flavored foods with full-bodied wines that can stand up to their pungent ingredients, and subtler foods with more delicate wines.

Hearty reds such as Argentinean Malbecs, Italian Barolos, Zinfandels, or California Cabernets are all logical accompaniments for well-seasoned meats. Medium-bodied reds like a French burgundy or a California Pinot Noir (both made from the same grape) are most suitable for milder flavors, such as a simply prepared piece of salmon or an herb-roasted chicken. For white wines, a crisp, dry Sauvignon Blanc or French Chablis will cut through shellfish or seafoods that are naturally rich (e.g., scallops or lobster), or prepared with lots of butter, cream, or oil. California Chardonnays, often described as being "oaky" or "buttery," are able to hold their own when served with spicy dishes and can also provide a favorable foil for leaner foods, such as a simply prepared piece of fish or chicken, or simple grilled vegetables. German Rieslings are my favorite to pair with some of my spicier bites because their balanced fruitiness tempers the heat so nicely. And so on.

At a more advanced level of food-and-wine pairing, wines are selected for their natural levels of acidity, sweetness, and fruitiness to enhance or counterbalance the fats, sugars, salts, spices, and acids of the food they are paired with. There are so many guidelines that it is dizzying to try to digest them all at once—and some even seem to contradict each other. Many of the recipes in this book are accompanied by a wine recommendation. You can also wing it and let logic and instinct rule. Eventually, you will discover the combinations that appeal to you and gain the confidence to boldly go where no wine snob has gone before. One of my favorite pairings is a full-bodied Cabernet Sauvignon with a rich slice of chocolate cake.

don't get too chill

White wines are typically served well chilled (approximately 45°F/7°C). But too much chill can mask a wine's delicate characteristics. At the Los Angeles International Wine & Spirits Competition, where I have had the honor of being a judge for the past eight years, white wines are tasted at room temperature so that the flavors—and imperfections—are accentuated. The next time you are drinking a nice glass of white, observe how its characteristics change as it warms up in the glass. Ultimately, the perfect temperature is the one that's perfect for you.

breathe

There is a lot of mystique attached to the rituals of decanting wines and letting them "breathe." It is true that older red wines do tend to blossom in flavor and complexity after they are uncorked and left to stand. But for any wine to breathe properly, it must be poured out of the bottle, because the amount of surface area at the neck doesn't expose enough of the juice to the air. At home, I pour the first two glasses and let them sit while I am cooking. This simplified version of decanting allows the wine in the glasses, as well as what remains in the bottle, time and room to hyperventilate to its heart's content. Even if you don't do anything, a wine will "open up" as you drink your way through the bottle. Becoming conscious of the subtle changes is the next level of awareness.

The other reason for decanting is to filter out the sediment that may develop in older wines. If you are lucky enough to be drinking such a wine, keep it stationary for at least an hour. Then steadily pour it into a carafe or pitcher, being careful to trap the sediment in the last few drops of wine—which you should leave in the bottle.

work on your timing

At tastings, wines are usually served in order from lightest and youngest to oldest and boldest. This rule should be followed only as long as the taste buds remain sober. Avoid the temptation to uncork treasured bottles at the end of a night of heavy drinking—despite the inevitability that the idea will seem inspired at the time (and trust me, no one will attempt to discourage you). Save your most treasured wines for those who will appreciate them. To weed out anyone who would have preferred white Zinfandel but was afraid to ask, use the following multiple-choice quiz: Cabernet is a) a new Volkswagen convertible, b) a piece of French furniture, c) an aromatic, deeply colored grape, or d) a trendy New York dance club.

age gracefully

Fine red wines continue to improve with age as their tannins soften and their complexities develop. Heat, vibration, dry air, and light are their enemies as they mature. They should be stored on their side in a still, dark, humid place at a constant temperature of about 55°F (13°C). That said, 99 percent of all wine produced today is ready to drink the second it hits the shelves. Unless you plan to hold on to a bottle for more than a year, just keep it in a cool part of the house, out of direct sunlight, and away from vibrating beds.

keep it clean

In the short lifespan of stemless glasses (like the Riedel "O" series), I have gone from mocking them to praising them for their fineness and functionality. Regardless of if you are drinking from thin crystal stemware or empty baby jars (been there, done that), make sure your glassware is completely free of soap and other residues. Often, glasses that look clean to the eye actually have traces of dishtowel or dishwasher smell. And even perfectly clean glasses have some ambient smell. That's why upscale restaurants buff their glasses with a clean linen napkin before setting them on the table, and why at fine wine tastings, glasses are "rinsed" with a small amount of the wine that is being served before the wine is poured.

shop around

There is a proverb in the art world that states if a work of art isn't selling, double the price. In my travels, I have been privy to conversations revealing that certain winemakers inflate their prices substantially, as a marketing ploy. Gaga reviews and over-the-top ratings by wine demigods like Robert Parker, and in magazines like *Wine Spectator*, can also drive the price of a wine well beyond its true market value. Ignore the hype and search for a similar wine with an inferior publicist.

There are many other ways to stretch your wine budget. In your search for affordable, easy-drinking wines, let others do the legwork for you. A good place to discover bargain wines is at restaurants that have a designated "house" wine. Such wines are usually selected for their good value and broad appeal. If you like it, ask to see the label. Or stay at home and experiment. The same $20 that buys the least expensive selection on a restaurant wine list (make that $25 after tax and tip) will help you procure a fine specimen in the wine shop.

don't expect it to feel like the first time

The company (especially a dream date), occasion, surroundings, and accompanying food can have more influence on your lingering memory of a wine than the juice itself. To avoid disappointment, don't expect an identical bottle to ring the same bells it did the first time. That said, if you ever taste an exceptional wine and decide to track down another bottle, don't allow yourself to be steered to another year of the same wine, or another wine of the same year and region. Virtually every time I have let down my guard and broken this rule, I have been disappointed.

be impulsive

A special wine can create an occasion—you don't always have to wait for one. It's also important to learn when to ignore everything anyone (including me) has ever told you about wine protocol. Confucius says, "He who holds out too long for the perfect occasion, or the perfect guest, may leave behind many unopened bottles."

when in romanée ...

In 1999, during a "research" trip to Burgundy, France, I made it my mission to visit the Domaine de la Romanée-Conti, one of the world's most celebrated wineries. This was no easy feat since the Domaine is part of a rarefied group of winemakers who don't need to blow their own horns—or even give tours. In fact, no outsiders are permitted to visit. It took a letter of introduction from one of my wine gurus to get me through the fabled gates.

During my vineyard tour, the sight of happy pickers filled my head with the romantic notion of changing my plans and joining the harvest. I asked my tour guide, the winery's general manager, if I could "help out for a day or two." With thinly veiled amusement he told me that the vendangeurs *(grape pickers) were highly trained workers who came back year after year, and worked the entire harvest—which, roughly translated, means "I speet on your seely request." In a moment of foolish bravado, I tried to salvage my dignity by asking if I could come back the following year for the whole harvest. This only seemed to increase his amusement, but he gamely suggested that I should send him a fax detailing why I wanted to be a grape picker.*

It wasn't until I returned home that it dawned on me that I had fumbled my way into a rare opportunity that any oenophile would kill for—a glimpse into the inner sanctum of Domaine de la Romanée-Conti. The fact that I had to pick a few grapes while I was there seemed to be a small price to pay.

Picture yourself condemned to a chain gang, hunched over in the early morning mist, ankles deep in mud, and muscles screaming for mercy. A bell clangs, a tractor roars into view, and you hear corks pop. Around you, 64 aching bodies lay down their tools and converge around the tractor. In an instant, the world turns from black and white to Technicolor as you are handed a glass of chilled rosé and a Camembert sandwich. This is the constant cycle of agony and ecstasy that defines the life of a grape picker at Domaine de la Romanée-Conti (DRC).

Every year, for 10 days in September, an elite team of pickers arrive from near and far to harvest the precious fruit from the Domaine's mythical seven-parcel portfolio of vineyards. This year they allowed a novice to join the ranks. That novice was me.

The winery is located in the village of Vosne-Romanée (population: 350), nestled within the Côte de Nuits wine-producing region of Burgundy, 20 miles south of Dijon. The Domaine's holdings include six adjacent tiny plots of land and one additional satellite plot 30 miles away in the revered white wine–producing region of Puligny-Montrachet. Each vineyard has a different name and yields a distinctive, eponymously named wine: La Tâche, Richebourg, Romanée Saint-Vivant, Grand Echézeaux, Echézeaux, Montrachet, and the jewel in the crown, Romanée-Conti. The latter yields, on average, a mere 6,000 bottles annually, which retail for $1,500 each when they are released, and escalate exponentially with age. In fact, to purchase a single bottle of Romanée-Conti, retail stores must buy a mixed case of the Domaine's wines. It is so scarce and so expensive that few wine lovers actually get to experience it in their lifetime.

All seven of the Domaine's wines are Grand Crus—a designation irrevocably granted in 1939 to the top 2 percent of wine-producing properties in Burgundy. What distinguishes a Grand Cru property from other less worshipped plots is its terroir—an intangible concept best described as the harmonic convergence of soil, subsoil, sun, air, and the passing of wine-making je ne sais quoi from generation to generation.

But not all Grand Crus are created alike. Two things make DRC the king of Burgundies: the magical combination of skeletal limestone, clay, and lime-marble soil, which forces the vines to work harder, thereby generating a lower yield—but with infinitely more concentrated fruit; and the total lack of compromise used in transforming that fruit into wine.

They are not known to compromise on their grape pickers either, but for me they seem willing to make an exception—perhaps in the name of international diplomacy. In early July, I received a fax: "We are pleased to confirm that you will be part of our grape-picking team. Be prepared to arrive in Vosne-Romanée on September 10. PS, the date may change without notice, depending on the status of the ripening grapes." Like the winemakers themselves, I was at the mercy of the grape.

On September 14, after an 18-hour journey, I arrive in Vosne-Romanée. It's the kind of picture-perfect French village that you see on posters in travel agencies. Stone houses, narrow streets, geraniums in the window baskets, and only one shop, which, to put a finer point on it, is the front vestibule of someone's house.

My accommodation is a small, virtually unfurnished stone house owned by the Domaine and located 20 feet from its front gates. My tiny room has a bare lightbulb and a narrow bed with a sagging mattress—a scary thought considering the backbreaking work ahead, not to mention the delicate condition of my two recently herniated discs. Upstairs, in an equally bare room, is an oenology student with whom I share a kitchen table and a bathroom without a door. I am feeling positively monklike in these Spartan surroundings until I learn that they are downright luxurious in comparison to the accommodations of the other 20 boarders, who are housed three to a room on folding cots. And even that is lavish in comparison to what awaits many pickers at the surrounding châteaux who, after a grueling day in the fields, come home to a tent. Grape picking and camping—the French equivalent of a biathlon.

That night, I fall into a coma at 11 p.m., then wake up completely disoriented to the loud clanging of a bell at 2 a.m. From my open window I spot the source: a large church steeple, just 55 yards away. For the rest of the night, on the half hour, the bell reverberates loudly. Between my jet lag and the noise, sleep is not an option. With nothing to do but read, I fully digest *Romanée-Conti: The World's Most Fabled Wine* by Richard Olney—a fascinating study of the Domaine's properties, beginning with its ownership by the Saint-Vivant de Vergy monastery in the 17th century.

At 7 a.m. I roll out of bed, barely refreshed by my three hours of sleep, but extremely well informed about my surroundings. I wander to the dining hall at the Domaine building, where coffee, cocoa, bread, and jam are set out. Then I am invited into the office of Gerard, the field manager. He gives me a toothy smile as he equips me with a pair of tall rubber work boots, a hand clipper, a green rubber rain suit, and a pannier (a plastic basket). The pickers congregate outside of the garage that houses the tractors. The returning pickers greet each other warmly while the handful of new ones huddle among those they came with, or stand alone. I feel like a kid arriving at summer camp for the first time. At 7:45 we are led up a short gravel road, just past the famous stone cross that marks the Romanée-Conti plot. We take a brief right and suddenly row upon row of the neatly groomed vines of the Richebourg plot spread out before us. Gerard divides us into three teams. Each team comprises a specially designed tractor that straddles the rows of vines, a driver, two foremen, and 21 pickers. I am intentionally placed between four veteran pickers, all women.

Just then a tall, willowy, gentle-mannered man enters the scene. It is Aubert de Villaine, the third-generation co-owner and patriarch of the winery. Aubert says hello to the familiar faces and welcomes new ones, shaking hands with the men and kissing the women on both cheeks.

Gerard positions each of us in front of our own row of vines, like sprinters in their lanes. The church clock strikes 8, Aubert shouts, *"Allez, courage,"* and we start picking. Gerard gives me a crash course on how and what to pick, then he leaves me to my own devices.

Unlike Napa and other warm wine-producing regions of the world where the trellises are at chest level, the grapes in Burgundy are trained to hang 6 to 18 inches from the ground. This allows them to absorb the warmth of the soil at night, thereby avoiding the perils of frost during the colder part of the growing season. Contrary to popular belief and the dire warnings of my friends, picking is not about the back as much as it is the thighs, which bear all the weight as one squats down in front of the vines.

The picking routine is as follows: The right hand acts as a weed whacker, ripping the lower leaves off the vines and exposing the hanging grape bunches. Then the left hand swoops in with the clippers. On some vines, the deep purple grapes dangle in multiple tiny clusters,

requiring the dexterity and finesse of a precision hairdresser. On others, they hang in large bunches, and with three or four snips, the vine is bared.

Before each bunch is placed in the pannier, the picker must eyeball it and, if necessary, trim off any sections of the bunch that are rotten or dried out. Depending on the microclimate and the year, this can be either a cursory or very time-consuming task. Not every grape cluster is picked. On some vines, a second, latent growth appears. These grapes are similar in color to the desirable ones, but they are younger and their acidity levels are way too high. Sometimes they are easy to differentiate, but other times the only way to know for sure is to bite into one and do a quick sugar analysis on the fly before shuffling like a crab to the next vine.

About every 15 minutes, someone fills their basket and shouts, "Pannier." On cue, all of the other pickers stand up in their lane and fall into line with military precision. Then the panniers and their 25 pounds of fruit loot are hoisted up and passed over the vines like water buckets at a fire, until they reach the tractor. The two foremen on the tractor gently empty the grapes into shallow, plastic boxes that are designed to stack up on each other without squishing any of the precious cargo. The empty panniers are passed back, the pickers return to work, and the grapes are ferried to a flatbed truck that transports them to the vinification room. There they are placed on a conveyor belt, where a team of 10 men weeds out the undesirable grapes that the vendangeurs have overlooked. The remaining grapes continue along the conveyor belt, through a machine that partially de-stems them. From there they are carried into another piece of equipment that lightly crushes them. Finally, they are dropped into a giant wooden cask, where they are left to macerate and ferment.

The *vendange* is executed like a military exercise. Vines are counted off, and pickers are assigned to rows in the same order every time. Sometimes, without warning, we are marched to other parts of the vineyard. Later, I learn that the winemakers gather before dinner in a war room to taste vineyard samples, study analyses, and decide which parcels of grapes are ready to be picked and which ones require more hang time.

At the clang of 9 a.m., work in the field comes to an abrupt halt. I have only been on the job for one hour but I already have a sense of what lies ahead of me, and I'm pathetically grateful for the break. We leave our panniers in our respective rows and congregate by an old stone wall at the end of the vines. Paper-wrapped packets are distributed. Each one contains a hunk of bread with a thick slab of sausage (on alternating days the bread contains a wedge of Camembert cheese). It is always accompanied by two sticks of dark chocolate, which I eat on the first day, then eventually learn to squirrel away for a much-needed late afternoon pick-me-up. Bottles are uncorked and rosé is poured freely (I rarely drink before noon, but when in Romanée . . .). It's an energy-boosting breakfast that could only have been designed by a French nutritionist. We lean against the wall, literally and figuratively chewing the fat. Virtually all the pickers fire up a postmeal Gitanes, then it's time to return to work. "Allez, courage."

We continue picking until 11 a.m., when thankfully it's time for a quick cigarette break. Never has a nonsmoker supported the habit with such enthusiasm. During this brief respite, everyone stays in their respective alleys, leaning over the vines to converse like neighbors gossiping over a fence.

At 11:25, the first grape picker goes down for the count. After severing the tip of his thumb with an errant snip of his clippers, a young German college student became dizzy and subsequently fainted. A crowd gathers around him for a minute as he is revived and bandaged up, then the rest of us get back to picking. The distractions of the morning begin to fade. My quad muscles are cramping and my back is twitching in pain. I've run four marathons and I've cycled one hundred miles in a day, but neither compares to the physical demands of grape picking. They told me to bring lots of sunscreen, but BENGAY would have been more appropriate. The next 30 minutes feel like hours, then the clock clangs 12 times, and with a collective sigh of relief we head in for lunch.

After hosing the mud off our boots, the 65 of us, along with the rest of the Domaine's workers, seat ourselves at four long vinyl-covered tables. Each place is set with a plate, a Duralex glass tumbler, a knife, and a fork. The plate is used for all four courses and the glass for water, wine, and coffee.

I am about to discover the paradox of the vendange: hours of physical punishment are juxtaposed with pure, hedonistic pleasure. Along the center of each table are four unlabeled wine bottles and four pitchers of water. I gulp down some much-needed water, then pour myself a glass of wine. It is a soft wine with oodles of up-front fruit, primarily raspberry, and a long lingering finish that defies its humble designation as a *vin de table*. Most châteaux bottle their best juice for their signature wines, then package the rest under another label, which is sold as their second wine. Later on, I learn that at DRC, what is not used for their seven legendary labels is blended into a wine that is served in-house. For the entire duration of the vendange, this luscious wine flows freely at lunch and dinner.

Lunch begins with tomato salad topped with crumbled egg, shallots, and a pungent Dijon vinaigrette. The room hums as the conversation builds and everyone unwinds. The rudimentary French of my Canadian upbringing saves me from being left in the cold, and I am swept up in the warmth of the atmosphere. Each new course arrives looking like it was plucked from the glossy cover of a food magazine. The entrée is a meaty peasant stew served over couscous. It's followed by the traditional cheese course, and the meal ends with an apple tarte tatin with a flaky, buttery crust. The food is all prepared by a husband and wife catering team from nearby Nuits-Saint-Georges who come every year to cook for the vendangeurs. Three women, including the indefatigable Charlotte, a tiny, wiry woman who has been working at the Domaine for 23 years, ferry the family-style platters to the table and—more importantly—replenish them.

After lunch we lounge on the grass outside and the omnipresent cigarettes are lit. The morning haze has burned off and the warm sun massages my pained legs. Just as I doze off, the clock tower clangs 1:30, sending us back to the fields. "Allez, courage."

In the afterglow of the wine-filled meal, the first hour of squatting, clipping, and lifting passes rather easily. But the buzz wears off and the pain returns—and intensifies. The golden sunshine of the morning has turned into a punishing midday heat. Layers of clothes are peeled off and reconfigured as makeshift sun hats. Two hours later, my quads have permanent charley horses, and the strength in my upper body is so drained that I can barely hoist the panniers to hip level in order to pass them over the vines. It dawns on me that I have another seven days of this. I seriously contemplate throwing myself under the wheels of the tractor.

The church bell clangs again, bringing me back to reality. My nighttime nemesis has become my new best friend as it slowly counts off the hours. I am obviously not doing a good job of masking my pain since the women around me motheringly ask, "*Ce n'est pas trop dur?*" and motion to the foreman to get me some rosé. I drag my sorry ass along the seemingly endless rows of vines until the single bell at 5:30 mercifully puts an end to my misery.

I limp back to my house. I am dying for a long hot bath with Epsom salts. Well, this may be an oenophile's paradise, but it ain't no spa. My shower is a two-foot by two-foot stall with a hand nozzle that has no attachment to hook onto. I wash the mud and dried, sticky grape juice from my punished body, then dry myself with a washcloth. I collapse onto my cot for an hour before dinner.

Dinners are a more intimate affair than lunches, attended only by the 20 pickers who are being housed at the Domaine. Those who live within driving range have all gone home. We gather at one table, where the wine and water sit in their familiar places. With my first sip of wine, the pleasure/pain pendulum swings back into the pleasure zone. We start with onion soup served with crème fraîche, followed by beef Stroganoff. Over the course of the 10 days, we are also treated to salads of carrots, beans, beets, greens, tomatoes—almost always with the now-familiar Dijon mustard vinaigrette. The entrées are all classic French dishes such as beef bourguignon, roasted chicken halves au jus, and *tartiflette*, a crowd favorite made from boiled potatoes, lardons, and caramelized onions, topped with an entire Reblochon cheese and baked into a hearty gooey mess (see recipe page 243).

Sleep comes easy on my tiny mattress. The next time I hear the church bells, they clang seven times, and the cycle of pleasure and misery starts all over again.

By the third day, my fingernails are gnarled and thick with dirt. My cuticles are stained purple and my hands, especially my weed-whacking hand, is scratched from the vines and full of gashes where my clippers have cut through the vines and continued into my flesh. My ability to wield a chef's knife is in jeopardy, not to mention my future hand-modeling career.

But after another day, the pain starts to become manageable and I begin to find my groove in the fields. Over time, one develops an economy of movement and a sixth sense about which leaves the wayward bunches of grapes are lurking behind. And the individual grapes become less precious as I begin to grasp the bigger picture. All 63 acres must be picked quickly in order to avoid the threat of rain, which will further exacerbate the *pourriture* (rot) that already exists on many of the clusters. Eventually a bit of triage is required to decide how much time it is worth spending in order to save one-eighth of a bunch of grapes.

I am beginning to be able to take my eyes off my clippers and appreciate the splendor of my surroundings. The blue skies, rolling hills, and endless vines are hypnotic. The serenity of the countryside is interrupted only by the distant purr of passing trains and the occasional sonic roar of French fighter planes from the Dijon base flying their maneuvers overhead.

I am also moving beyond pleasantries and getting to know my fellow pickers. In the less-coveted *appellation côntrolée* vineyards, the pickers mostly comprise transient workers.

At DRC, they are college students, people who work in banks, real estate offices, lingerie stores, and shipyards. Some are grandmothers and grandfathers (including one grandmother who has picked for 22 years). Most are French, with a few stragglers from neighboring countries. The majority are on vacation time, and many told me that picking grapes helps them participate in, and connect with, this vibrant element of French culture. Everybody says that they come for the camaraderie. Consequently, there are no Walkmans or mirrored wraparound sunglasses. During the entire vendange, I only once heard a cell phone ring in the field.

By midweek everyone is catching their wind. The boarders start congregating after dinner in the nearby Saint-Vivant monastery, where several of them are squatting. Jojo, one of the foremen staying there, has a guitar and requires little encouragement to use it. The others sip Pernod, Scotch, or beer and sing along to traditional Burgundian songs.

In the village of Vosne-Romanée, there are approximately 40 châteaux, all of which produce wine from grapes grown in their respective vineyards, which surround the village. The teams of pickers at these châteaux are as distinctive as the wines they produce. I experience this first-hand one night while weaving home from a docile sing-along with the Domaine's pickers. In the darkness, a U2 song echoed through the stone-lined streets. Starved for some familiar music, I follow the sound to a nearby château, where I stick my head in to investigate and engage in a brief conversation with the wobbling, red-faced man leaning closest to the door. He tells me that he and his friends are celebrating their *paulée* (the traditional end-of-vendange party), which had begun 11 hours earlier, at noon. My bad French accent immediately gives me away as a foreigner, and I am invited in and presented with a glass of the château's '82 vintage. In the glow of my good fortune, I wander onto the dance floor. No sooner do I start dancing than a French novelty song that was a momentary hit the previous summer is tossed on the CD player. The lyrics in the chorus demand that all men take off their shirts. Without warning, my sweater is lifted over my head and I am standing half naked amidst a group of totally schnockered Frenchmen.

The revelry continues for another two hours. As we drink our way through several of that château's finer vintages, I become fast friends with a couple of the pickers. We close the party and continue drinking at a nearby house. At three in the morning, I beg off and stumble back to my mattress.

After four hours of sleep, my head throbs as I plod from vine to vine in the cold and drizzly morning. My newly acquired skills elude me. Without saying a word, the women on either side of me surreptitiously snip away at the grapes in my row, allowing me to keep pace. To compound my self-inflicted suffering, the drizzle turns to rain.

Then by the grace of God and the declaration of Aubert de Villaine (almost the same thing), the picking is halted after an hour and a half. When it rains, most vineyards keep picking. But at DRC, Aubert doesn't want the residual water covering the grapes and the droplets trapped amidst the tightly bunched clusters diluting the intensity of the wine. Hallelujah. My first instinct is to sleep. However, a primal need, one that Maslow neglected to include in his hierarchy, takes over: laundry. Every single piece of clothing I own is stained and sticky. I hitch a ride to Nuits-Saint-Georges. As my clothes tumble in the Laundromat, I wander off in

search of a pair of rubber gloves. Since both of my tender and scarred hands are performing completely different tasks, I buy a pair of thick rubber gloves for my weed-whacking hand and a thin, more responsive pair to use on my cutting hand. Note to self: in my next life, return as a rubber-glove magnate and create a special package of intentionally mismatched gloves for the grape-picking industry.

After a day off and a full night's sleep, I spring out of bed with renewed energy. A big orange sun rises over the horizon. To add to the pleasure, we are picking the Grand Echézeaux plot. This borders Clos de Vougeot, a cluster of famous Grand Cru plots surrounding a postcard-perfect château and enclosed by an ancient stone wall. Life is sweet.

Through observation and some lessons in broken French, I learn tricks of the trade that ease my transition from dilettante to seasoned picker. For instance, squeezing the tiny, unripened grape clusters that grow at the top of the vine produces a juice that's all acid and no sugar—perfect for cleaning sticky hands and sterilizing small cuts. And when my energy wanes, I learn to replenish it with grapes that are so brimming with sugar that they taste like tiny bonbons.

The tactile experience of being so close to the grapes also helps clarify some of the theories and mysteries of wine. In the fields it is not uncommon to have a 60-year-old vine with its thick, gnarled trunk growing beside a spry young specimen. In theory, older vines produce fewer, but more concentrated, grapes. Some wineries bottle wines from older vines under the label "*vielles vignes*" and charge a premium. Sampling grapes from both vines reveals a subtle, yet distinguishable, difference in sweetness and concentration.

And during a walk around at dusk through the different vineyards, the temperatures and humidity differ noticeably. These micro-microclimates affect everything from rot to the sweetness of the grapes. It is easy to understand how one wine can be so different from another produced in an adjacent vineyard.

Another three vineyards away, less than 435 yards from the DRC plots, lie the much less distinguished Vosne-Romanée appellation côntrolée vineyards. These vineyards produce wines that are good but not exceptional (partly because the terroir of the flat land is not as good as the sloped areas, and partly because the grapes are not as pampered at every step in the winemaking process). The next time a wine clerk tries to sell you a wine from a producer who is located "just down the road" from another (usually more prestigious) producer, don't let the association by proximity fool you.

The days fly by and the mood loosens in the fields. On the morning of the seventh day of picking, word spreads that only one more day remains—and more importantly, that the paulée will be held on Sunday at noon. By design, the paulées always begin at noon to give the pickers time (in theory) to sober up before the drive home.

Sensing that the end is near, the natives begin to grow restless. Whereas the occasional chiding grape was thrown around between pickers all week long, now whole bunches shuttle through the air. And the occasional playful squirts of water have turned into complete Vittel showers. I am given diplomatic immunity from most of the guerilla warfare—that is, until the end of the last day, when no one is spared.

Even at this late point in the harvest, when the legs and back have grown strong, there is a certain level of discomfort and monotony that sets in after a two-hour stretch of picking. Speculation about the wines to be served at the impending paulée provides the perfect distraction. Although everyone knows that the feast customarily includes a selection of vintage holdings from the cellar, the question on everyone's minds is which of the Domaine's wines and—more importantly—which vintages will Aubert choose? The veteran pickers raise the hope that he may dust off some bottles from the precious Romanée-Conti plot itself, as he is rumored to have done in the past.

On Friday, our last day, several of the older women bring homemade coffee cakes and beignets that they unwrap and share with us at the 9 a.m. break. Spirits are high, and I have finally hit my grape-picking stride (although perhaps it's the sugar rush). For the first time since we started, I fill my basket first and am able to utter the word that has eluded me for the whole week. "Pannier!" I cry triumphantly. A spontaneous, heartfelt applause breaks out among my fellow pickers.

Later that afternoon, Gerard places us in front of our final row of grapes. There is a buzz in the field and it's easy to tell that something is afoot. An hour later, as the last round of panniers is being passed along the fire line, all hell breaks loose. Suddenly bunches of grapes are flying in every direction and being squashed down every imaginable piece of clothing. It begins with the rejected clusters that the warriors pick off the ground, but quickly progresses to the panniers, and finally to a raid of the grapes that have already been loaded onto the tractors. It's like a food fight in a Sevruga caviar packing plant. I am sorry to report that several cases of precious Echézeaux were sacrificed in the traditional end-of-vendange battle.

After the free-for-all ends and the testosterone levels subside, we load our grape-stained bodies onto the tractors and flatbed trucks and ride in a convoy, with horns honking, for a victory lap around the village. Stray grapes fly at anybody within range. And it ain't over yet. As we reach home, the ringleaders leap off the tractor, commandeer the pressure hose that we use to clean the mud from our boots, and turn it on us. Everybody, including the foremen, is thoroughly drenched. Those foolish enough to try to make a break for it are quickly chased down and doused. Even Aubert de Villaine and his wife are caught in the melee, and he gamely returns fire. Only then is everyone prepared to call it quits and head to the showers.

Later that night, I leave a party at the monastery of Saint-Vivant. Nostalgically savoring my last glass of the table wine I've grown so fond of, I wander up to the cross at the Romanée-Conti plot. In the darkness, I see the vague outline of several lone individuals. A familiar voice calls out my name, and I realize that like me, my fellow pickers are paying homage to the grape gods. I lie down on the stone wall beneath the cross. Its sharp outline is silhouetted against the magical star-filled sky, adorned with the brightest Big Dipper I have ever seen. This is how the grapes of DRC spend their nights.

Had I been told after that first grueling day that I would be sad when the end arrived, I wouldn't have believed it—in fact, the mere concept of finishing the week alive seemed unfathomable at the time. But when the paulée finally arrives, it is bittersweet.

Everyone converges at the Domaine at noon, scrubbed, groomed, and full of anticipation. After an aperitif of Crémant (the local sparkling wine) and some pâté canapés, the dining hall doors open to reveal an amazing transformation. The familiar lunch tables have been dressed up with white tablecloths and bowls of wild flowers. In place of the Duralex tumblers are beautiful tulip-shaped crystal wineglasses. We enter with reverence and take our seats.

The first course is *feuilletté d'escargots à la crème d'oseille* (snails served in a puff pastry with a creamed herb sauce). After welcoming everyone and applauding them for completing a difficult picking season, Aubert introduces the first wine, an '87 Puligny-Montrachet. It has a deep golden, almost Sauternes-like color. The nose is all honey. It glides down the throat and perfectly complements the escargot. To my surprise, after our table finishes our two bottles, another one magically appears. Not a bad start.

Two huge magnums of '88 La Tâche are placed on the table to accompany the main course of filet mignon. I am astonished by the generosity—each one of these would fetch $1,000 from collectors. After spending eight days communing with the red grapes, touching them, nibbling them, and breathing in their aroma, the foreplay is finally over. It's time to consummate the relationship. I bury my nose in the glass and inhale its intense bouquet, then close my eyes and take a sip. Its viscosity is much thinner than I had imagined. The predominant impression is sour cherry, and the finish goes on and on. It is a great . . . a very great wine, but not transcendent.

As we finish the entrée, Aubert leaves his seat and walks into the kitchen. From my vantage point, I see him pull eight dusty bottles from a wooden crate. After carefully opening each bottle, he pauses to taste it, like a sommelier. Could this mean . . . ?

Cheese trays are passed around. Finally Aubert emerges. With obvious pleasure he announces that we are being served 1961 Romanée-Conti. A hush descends upon the room. I had dared to dream that I might taste a Romanée-Conti, but never a vintage as rare and priceless as this. A bottle is placed on our table, and when it makes its way to me, I cradle it in my hands. A considerable amount of sediment is evident at the bottom around the punt. I pour the precious liquid into my glass carefully and hold it up to the light. It is deep crimson in color, with shades of burned umber. On the nose, it has an intense, explosive aroma of such opulence that I am dazzled. I pause for a minute to meditate on its heady perfume, then I take my first sip. The wine dances on my tongue. It's an exhilarating sensation. I have had wines that were more instantly gratifying, but never one that was as complex and intellectually stimulating. The pleasure is, of course, enhanced by my intimate knowledge of its heritage. Minutes later, it gets even more sublime as it opens up in the glass. We are all acutely aware of the privilege that Aubert has bestowed upon us. A wine that serious collectors would kill for is being shared with 65 glorified field hands. The meal is capped off with a rich *gâteau au chocolat* and a round of the Domaine's Marc (a rough, cognaclike spirit distilled from pressed grape skins). Then abruptly, it's all over.

We all exchange addresses and say our good-byes. Then I head to my room to pack my bags for the flight home to Los Angeles. In another 18 hours, I will be back in a fast-paced world full of familiar faces, creature comforts, and fleeting moments of glamour. But now, that world seems daunting. How will I survive without the daily triumphs over sheer physical pain, the communing with nature, the camaraderie with absolutely no agenda, and the 9 a.m. rosé and Camembert sandwiches? Allez, courage.

traditional tartiflette

This interpretation of the classic French recipe was given to me verbally—to the best of my recollection—by André, the vendange caterer at Domaine de la Romanée-Conti. André served this insanely rich, deliciously gooey, savory mess as an entrée. If you haven't worked up a huge appetite from picking grapes for eight hours, I highly recommend you serve it as a side dish.

2 pounds (1 kg) potatoes (any variety will
   work)
2 tablespoons (30 mL) butter
1 onion, diced
6 ounces (175 g) lardons or pancetta
1 cup (250 mL) dry white wine
Salt and freshly ground black pepper to taste
¼ cup (60 mL) half-and-half cream (the French
   use heavy cream, but then, they put butter on
   their cheese)
1 Reblochon cheese or 12 ounces (375 g) of
   Muenster, Jarlsberg, or Swiss (in that order
   of preference)

Preheat oven to 350°F (180°C).

Peel potatoes and cut into ¼-inch-thick (6 mm) slices. Steam
potatoes until tender to the poke of a fork. Reserve.

In a heavy, large pan (ideally cast iron) over medium heat, melt butter and cook onion and lardons for approximately 6 minutes, or until they just begin to brown. Add potatoes and continue to cook for 10 more minutes.

Add the white wine and cook until it reduces by half.

Season pan contents generously with salt and pepper. If you are using a cast iron pan or any other ovenproof pan that you are happy to serve from, keep ingredients in pan. If not, butter a 10-inch (25 cm) baking dish, or close facsimile, and transfer the potato mixture to it. Pour the cream overtop. Cut Reblochon in half horizontally (if you are substituting a cheese that comes in block form, grate it coarsely). Place the halves of Reblochon on top, rind side up (or sprinkle grated cheese overtop), and bake for approximately 15 to 20 minutes, or until the cheese has melted into the potatoes. Serve immediately.

yield Serves 4 as an entrée, 6 to 8 as a side dish **uncommon goods** Reblochon cheese (available at specialty cheese shops) **level of difficulty** As easy as making mashed potatoes and a grilled cheese sandwich simultaneously. **active prep time** 40 minutes **inactive cooking time** 20 minutes **advance work** Can be prepped earlier in the day to the point that it is baked. **music to cook by** Django Reinhardt and Stéphane Grappelli, *Quintet du Hot Club de France*. Old-time speed jazz. **liquid assets** Anything from Domaine de la Romanée-Conti!, or any earthy red burgundy

fun
damentals
the basics and then some

Read the directions and directly you will be directed in the right direction.

—THE DOORKNOB, *Alice's Adventures in Wonderland*

fear of frying (a deep-frying tutorial)

Sure, deep-fried food is bad for us, but that's *exactly* why it tastes so good. When used judiciously, it can broaden your culinary repertoire and accent your menu with a pleasing crunch.

You don't need a deep fryer to deep-fry at home. I don't have one. All it takes is a deep pot or pan, some oil, and a healthy respect for a combustible liquid that is almost twice the temperature of boiling water.

equipment

☞ The ideal frying pot is a heavy, tall two-quart (2 L) pot. That said, most pots will work.

☞ The easiest way to maintain an ideal frying temperature (other than having a deep fryer) is to monitor the oil with an oil or candy thermometer—a worthy $20 investment.

☞ Fry baskets and Chinese spiders are handy, easy-on-the-pocketbook accessories for getting your food in and out of bubbling oil, but any slotted spoon will get the job done.

☞ If you get hooked on deep-fried pickles or Twinkies, you might consider investing in one of the many inexpensive consumer models of deep fryers available at cooking and department stores everywhere (and a gym membership!).

oil

☞ Peanut oil, with its high smoking point, is perfectly suited for deep-frying, but any vegetable oil can be used.

☞ The ideal oil depth for home frying is 2 to 3 inches (5 to 8 cm). Never fill the pot or pan more than one-third full. Oil has a tendency to bubble up vigorously as food is added.

☞ You can reuse the cooked oil several times. After each use, let the oil cool, then save it in the original bottle. Be sure to mark it as used so that you don't confuse it with your other oils. A $1 funnel will be your new favorite kitchen tool. And if you want to be really fancy, stick a bit of cheesecloth in the funnel to strain out the sediment. Store the used oil in a cool, dark place. You'll know your oil is spent when it starts smoking at the normal frying temperature, or when the color darkens substantially.

temperature

☞ The ideal frying temperature for the foods in this book is between 350°F and 360°F (177°C to 182°C). If the temperature is too high, food burns; too low, and it will be greasy. Depending on the amount of oil you are using and the amount and density of the food you are frying, the oil temperature will likely spike momentarily when you add the food, then drop as the frying process continues. Adjust your heat source accordingly to get back to 350°F (177°C) as quickly as possible.

☞ If you don't have an oil or candy thermometer, stick a ½-inch (1 cm) cube of bread on a fork and dip it in the hot oil. If the bread doesn't brown after 10 seconds, the oil is not hot enough. If the bread browns instantly, the oil temperature is too high. And if the bread turns into a golden crouton in 5 to 10 seconds, you are set to fry.

warning

Hot oil is verrrry dangerous. Never leave it unattended. And don't start drinking until after you have finished frying. The best way to put out an oil fire (God forbid) is to smother it with a tightly fitting lid. Or use a damp cloth to cover the flaming pan. Never throw water over burning oil, and never attempt to move a burning pan. There, now go fry away.

direct and indirect grilling techniques

direct grilling method

Direct grilling refers to grilling food directly over the heat source. On a gas grill, this means that all burners are lit. On a charcoal grill, it means that the coals are spread evenly on the bottom grate. As a rule of thumb, any food that cooks in 20 minutes or less should be grilled by the direct method. And foods that take longer than 20 minutes should be grilled by the indirect method or a combination of direct and indirect methods.

indirect grilling method

Indirect grilling means that the source of the heat cooking the food is not directly under the food. This cooking method requires a lid, which turns the grill into a convection oven. On a gas grill, depending on the number of burners it has, you need to turn off one or more of the burners that are directly under the food. On a charcoal grill, either push the coals to one side, or split them down the middle and push them to the sides of the grill.

clarifying butter

Butter browns, then burns, over high heat. When butter is clarified, it develops a higher smoke point because the milk solids, the part that browns, are removed.

To clarify butter, melt a minimum of a quarter pound (125 g) in a saucepan over low heat. When the butter is fully melted, remove from the heat and let stand for three minutes. The butter should settle into three layers: a frothy top, a clear yellow middle, and a milky solid bottom. Begin by skimming the froth off the top. Then carefully and slowly pour out the clear middle layer into a bowl while retaining all of the white solids in the saucepan. Discard the froth and solids. If necessary, repeat the skimming process on the contents in the bowl. Store clarified butter in an airtight container. It will last almost indefinitely in the refrigerator.

supreming citrus fruit

Supreming citrus fruit means removing the skin, pith, membranes, and seeds, and separating its segments into fruit fillets. To supreme any citrus, begin by cutting ¼ inch (6 mm) off each end. Then stand the fruit up on one end and slice off all the skin along with the outer membrane of the sections, thereby exposing the flesh. Hold the fruit in the palm of your hand, and use your knife to cut inside the membrane of each individual segment.

fire regulations (for flambéing)

☞ **clear the decks** To keep the flames from burning down the joint, clear the area of any flammable objects and move your fire extinguisher within easy reach.

☞ **cap it** If you have big rock-star hair, wear a hat.

☞ **reduce it** Too much liquid in the pan will dilute the alcohol and prevent it from igniting. Simmer the contents until no more than 2 to 3 tablespoons (30 to 45 mL) remain before adding the alcohol.

☞ **keep your distance** If you have a gas stove, be aware that spattering particles from the pan will likely cause the alcohol to ignite prematurely as soon as it is added.

☞ **put a lid on it** Keep a lid within easy reach. If the flames burn too high, or for more than 10 seconds, cover the pan with a lid.

life-affirming staples

olive oil

The olive oils used in Italy are so full of flavor that they are often used in place of sauce on grilled fish and pasta. Unfortunately, many of the oils selected and marketed for American tastes are intentionally less flavorful. A good rule of thumb is that deeper-colored olive oils are more complex and flavorful, but the only way to be sure is to taste test several varieties on small squares of bread (or just a spoon if you want the most accurate read). Some specialty food shops have sample tables so that you can try before you buy.

High-quality oils are exponentially more expensive, so I always keep two grades on hand. I use the best one where its rich, nutty flavor and peppery finish can be easily distinguished (i.e., on bread, on delicately flavored pasta, and in simple salad dressings). I use the inexpensive oil in most situations where it is being heated (i.e., sautéing), in marinades, and in all other situations where the subtleties are indistinguishable.

All oils contain the same amount of fat—even the so-called light oils. If you are trying to use less oil, use one that's more robust. A little goes a long way. Store your oil in a cool, dark place.

salt

It is easy to be skeptical about the ever-expanding salt universe. However, salt is just like olive oil and wine. Once you tune in to the subtle differences of the good stuff, it's hard to go back. Most chefs I know cook with kosher salt in their restaurants and their homes because it is free of additives and comes in a coarse form. They keep a small ramekin of it beside their prep station, and when the need arises to season with salt, they pinch a bit between their fingers. The feel of the salt grains is very pleasing to the touch, and it allows more control over the amount used.

For a difference you can taste, splurge on some *sel gris* or *fleur de sel*. These are hand-harvested from sea marshes on the west coast of France and are used as a finishing touch much like a fine olive oil. Sel gris, also known as *sel de Guérande*, is a coarse, grayish salt that is rich in minerals. It doesn't dissolve as soon as it comes into contact with food, so when you bite into its crystals on bruschettas, on vegetables (especially tomatoes and potatoes), or in salads, your mouth is filled with an intense explosion of flavor. Fleur de sel, the very top sun-bleached layer of sel gris, is exponentially more expensive.

These days, fancy sea salts come in a variety of forms and colors, and are available from all over the globe. I can't claim to be able to differentiate all of the subtle differences in flavor, but I do admit an infatuation with them. If you are curious, but not willing to fork out a large fortune for a small jar of salt, dip your toe in the ocean with a box of Maldon sea salt. At about $8 for eight ounces, these light salt flakes are well worth the price.

finishing touches

While doing a *stage* at Craft in New York City, I learned an intriguing chef trick that has had a lasting impact on me.

The entire kitchen at Craft is designed in a V formation. As each sous chef finishes preparing their component of a dish, they pass it down the line to the next station. The finished dishes are then funneled to the executive chef, who stands in his crisp chef whites at the front of the formation. He inspects each plate suspiciously, and frequently takes a spoon from his jacket pocket to sample a little morsel. Then he barks orders at the sous chef in charge of the inevitable travesty. (Gordon Ramsay would look like a pussycat next to this guy.) Regardless of whether the entrée is a piece of fish, steak, pasta, or a vegetable, he tops everything with a sprinkle of fine sea salt and a drizzle of fragrant olive oil that the restaurant imports directly from Italy. These final touches serve to envelop the customer's first bite with an unforgettable layer of richness and flavor.

whole black peppercorns

Freshly ground black pepper is a must in any serious kitchen. For a coarser grind, loosen the top screw of your pepper grinder. My favorite type of peppercorn is the Tellicherry. It is more expensive than other peppercorns but justifies its cost by delivering a stronger and more fragrant bite. To avoid being put through the mill yourself, buy peppercorns at bulk stores.

fresh herbs

Fresh herbs have a totally different personality from the dried variety. Their flavors are much more immediate, especially uncooked or when added in the final stages of cooking. Most large grocery stores now stock all the fresh herbs I call for in this book (cilantro, Italian parsley, rosemary, basil, oregano, thyme, mint, dill, tarragon, and sage). When cooking with these herbs, save some to add just before serving. This will "refresh" the flavor. If you are substituting dried herbs for fresh ones, a good rule of thumb is to use half of the required amount. Dried herbs benefit from heat, which helps to release their flavors. They should be added earlier in the cooking process than fresh herbs. Crushing them in your hand before using also helps to release their flavors.

garlic

Accept no substitute. When buying garlic, look for a firm bulb. As it gets older and moves past its prime, the bulb loses its firmness and green sprouts appear in each clove (although not ideal at this stage, both the clove and the sprout can still be used). If you like the taste of garlic but have problems digesting it, try a trick I picked up while loitering in a restaurant kitchen in Italy: instead of mincing the cloves, add one or two whole peeled cloves while cooking, then fish them out and discard before serving.

If raw garlic keeps vampires at bay, then it's a good bet that roasted garlic would make them give up their bloodsucking ways forever. Roasting garlic (see page 144) magically transforms each clove into a sweet, caramelized jewel that tastes nothing like the pungent bite of the raw stuff. Roasted garlic cloves are a great addition for pastas, salads, soups, risottos, and pizzas. Or simply spread a few cloves on a toasted baguette slice. Always make extra to keep on hand for these uses. Be forewarned: roasted garlic has an odiferous way of saying "hello" the next morning.

shallots and leeks

Both of these members of the onion family are more complex in flavor than the common cooking onion. When they are sautéed or baked slowly over moderate heat, their natural sugars are drawn out and caramelized. The result is a sweet, mild, almost unrecognizable version of their former selves that will add depth to sauces, sandwiches, burgers, soups, pastas, stuffings, salads, and potatoes.

lemons and limes

As obvious as it may seem, these old standbys are often forgotten. Their juice and zest are worth many times their actual cost.

fresh gingerroot

Fresh gingerroot can add a vibrant dimension to many meat and vegetable dishes. Select taut, bulbous pieces. Peel, and mince or grate finely when adding to marinades or soups. Slice it or use a coarser grater for use in woks or when you want to give the taste buds (and sinuses) a real kick. Gingerroot keeps for a couple of weeks in the refrigerator and shrivels when old. I recently learned a nifty trick from the gregarious Montreal chef Giovanni Apollo. If you want to add ginger juice to a sauce, salsa, or anything else, freeze a piece of gingerroot, then let it thaw. To juice it, simply squeeze the root in your hand over the dish.

current addictions

(still legal in most states and provinces)

chipotle chili

When I wrote *Off the Eaten Path*, few people were hip to chipotle. A decade later, there is a chain of Mexican fast-food restaurants that bears the same name. Chipotle chili is a Southwestern specialty made from jalapeño chilies that are smoked for days over aromatic woodcuttings. Its smoky campfire aroma imparts a distinctive spicy flavor to anything it is added to, especially salsas, chili, eggs, and dry rubs. It's so addictive that I carry a vial with me on the road to surreptitiously spice up bland meals. The dried version is available whole or ground. A canned version, pickled in adobo sauce, is available in many grocery stores.

parmigiano reggiano

Parmigiano Reggiano is the godfather of all Parmesan cheese. No other cheese tastes quite as rich and nutty as authentic Parmigiano Reggiano, which is made from the milk of specially fed cows and aged for two years. It is so addictive that I made a pilgrimage to Parma, Italy, to watch it being made. My curiosity was rewarded with an unforgettable lesson in old-world techniques and a three-pound wedge as a parting gift. Of the three million wheels produced every year, Italians consume a staggering 93 percent, leaving the rest of the world to fight over the remainder. It is so valuable that when Italian banks lend money to cheesemakers, they hold their 80-pound wheels in special vaults as collateral. At about $16 a pound, it's definitely pricey, but an affordable six-ounce wedge goes a long way. For the freshest Parmigiano Reggiano, purchase from stores that move a lot of it. To get the most cheese for your buck, go for a center-cut fillet, but no matter what, avoid pieces that have disproportionate amounts of rind.

A generous sprinkle of Parmigiano Reggiano, grated just before serving, enhances pastas, salads, and many soups. For extra punch, use a coarser grater or wide shavings. To fully appreciate its distinctive qualities, chip off a nugget-size piece and eat it on its own.

prosciutto

Prosciutto is the salt-cured, air-dried hind leg of a pig, traditionally served in paper-thin slices. The good stuff is cured for over a full year and has a unique flavor and texture that melts in your mouth. At about $20 a pound ($4.50/100 g), it's expensive—but worth every penny. True prosciutto is from the area around Parma, Italy—not coincidentally the same region where they make Parmigiano Reggiano. The pigs are fed whey, a by-product of the cheesemaking process. France and Spain also produce great variations, known as *jambon de Bayonne* and *jamón serrano*, respectively. To up the ante, some of these pigs are allowed to graze in oak forests, where they gorge on acorns. Sadly, these versions of prosciutto are not widely available outside of Europe. I have tasted many North American products, and with the exception of a few tiny artisanal producers, I *speeet* on them all.

pancetta

Pancetta is an Italian bacon that is cured with salt and spices—but is not smoked. It can be found in a 4-inch-diameter (10 cm) sausagelike roll in most Italian food shops and at many specialty butchers. Ask for slices ⅛ inch (3 mm) thick. Cut it crosswise into ¼-inch (6 mm) strips, fry it like bacon, and add it to pastas, eggs, and salads.

maple syrup

As a child growing up in Montreal, I used to tap the maple tree in our front yard every spring and boil the sap in my mother's kitchen. This inevitably led to a very sticky kitchen ceiling and one measly cup of syrup. We used it on pancakes and French toast. Now, I am equally likely to include maple syrup in dressings, marinades—and even in my ice cream (see page 160). Fortunately, the global grocery store has made it available worldwide. Grade AA is the lightest, most delicate variety, but I highly recommend the darker grades, which tend to be more flavorful, and less expensive.

how-to diagrams

Lettuce Leaves Salmon (page 126)

Bang Bang Drummettes (page 68)

Chinese/Ahi Sno-Cones (page 48/51)

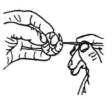

Coconut Shrimp Lollypops (page 54)

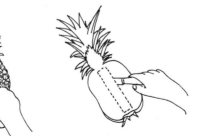

Lucky Duck
(page 114)

Tuna Fish 'n' Chips
(page 66)

Existential Eggs (page 220)

1. Slice bottom off egg.

2. Pipe mousse into shell.

3. Press frozen passion fruit yolk into mousse.

4. Pipe mousse over yolk to ¼" (1 cm) from top.

5. Fill remaining space with melted chocolate.

6. Serve in an eggcup.

Pyrotechnic Pineapple (page 152)

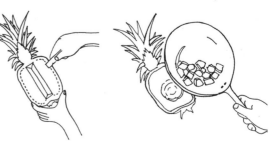

after words

closing
thoughts

There are some days when I think I am going
to die from an overdose of satisfaction.

—SALVADOR DALÍ

resolutions for a personal culinary revolution

HERE ARE A FEW CULINARY RESOLUTIONS that will help you get a lot more out of life—regardless of what your lot in life is.

buy the farm Shop at farmers' markets. Many of the vendors at farmers' markets are the farmers themselves. These salt-of-the-earth souls grow produce for flavor, not appearance and shipping endurance—and they're proud of it. Ask them for cooking tips, storage suggestions, or recipes, and you're bound to expand your culinary horizons.

be daring Try a food you've hated all your life. If you still makes you squirm, you're that much braver for having tried it.

get real Use fresh rather than processed or artificially flavored ingredients. Buy real lemons instead of plastic ones, whole garlic bulbs, fresh herbs, and vegetables off the stem. When time permits, honor your taste buds by taking a few minutes to make common convenience foods from scratch. Mash your own guacamole, squeeze your own orange juice, and bake your own cookies.

linger longer The French mock us for our lack of sophistication, then eat and drink whatever they want—and have the last laugh by outliving the average North American. Medical researchers have attributed this feat to miracle-working components contained in red wine, and have dubbed it the French Paradox. My personal theory is that the French style of lingering and laughing around the dinner table minimizes the stress on the digestive system and allows the body to concentrate on more important business.

be sinful Take pleasure—not guilt—in eating something sinful. If it makes you happy, it's good for you (in moderation).

start a food fight Send your food back in restaurants when it's not right. Remember, it's a service industry and you are there to be accommodated, not intimidated. (Notable exception: don't piss off the knife-wielding chefs at Benihana.)

be complimentary Praise the chef when the food is exceptional. Even if it's just a humble pancake joint, walk into the kitchen and pay homage.

undress the emperor Determine for yourself which brands are better—not just better marketed—by conducting your own blind tasting. Blind-tasting beverages (e.g., packaged juice, vodka, mineral water) or food products (e.g., chocolate, pasta sauce, olive oil) is fun to do with friends and inevitably produces results that are surprising.

upgrade Bring your own food on airplanes. If you're a champagne flyer traveling on a (honey-roasted) peanut budget, make a difference you can actually taste by packing a bag with the following: a take-out dinner from your favorite restaurant, some snacks (i.e., candy bars, fresh-baked cookies, fresh fruit, trail mix, gummy bears) and your favorite herbal or specialty tea bags. Avoid any sauces, dips, or condiments that could possibly be misconstrued as weapons of mass destruction.

be cheesy Frequent a cheese shop and discover the difference between cheese and C-H-E-E-S-E.

be enlightening Use candles to illuminate routine weekday dinners.

accent the positive Splurge on some fancy sea salt, and use it to add a bright accent to your dishes.

drink less, but drink better As you climb the wine and spirits ladder, let quality replace quantity.

be more spontaneous Throw a dinner party—just for the hell of it. Whether it's as mundane as the February blues, a full moon, or a cost-of-living raise, there's always an excuse to invite friends over, toss together an impromptu meal, and dust off a few bottles of wine.

become a man or woman for all seasons Eat with the seasons. If you avoid flown-in produce, the wait will make the local variety taste that much sweeter when it is finally ripe for the picking.

plant the seeds of change Grow something. A shovelful of dirt and a couple of pots is all it takes. If you have a brown thumb, start with mint, rosemary, and thyme—you can't kill them if you try.

be giving Make an annual donation of time, energy, or money to a food bank. If you are capable of incorporating even a few of these resolutions into your routine, chances are that you are in a position to help those less fortunate than yourself.

outro

Over the course of my journey, I have become the poster child for the adage "If you love what you do, you will never work a day in your life." And I am the ultimate testament to what parents always try to instill in their children—that we are all capable of being anything we want to be.

I am constantly inspired by the chefs whom I count as friends. And I get inspired by inspiring others, whether it's sharing tips in person, on the Internet, or over the airwaves. I still get excited when I learn about new ingredients, wander through farmers' markets around the globe, discover new wine varietals, and observe new tricks and cooking techniques.

Although I am sometimes stubborn and single-minded in my focus (some might say pigheaded), I've retained the essence of every lesson I have learned during my culinary career. At this point, I am a pastiche of the knowledge of the chefs, writers, restaurateurs, winemakers, and savants I have met and collaborated with along the way. I've learned how to perfectly poach an egg, and how to catch a catfish with my bare hands. I've also learned a lot about people: that just below the surface of the average Joe often lies a burning passion for food or an obscure culinary skill; and that many experts and champions who have been doing things the same way forever can be beaten by a newcomer with a fresh perspective (and a healthy dose of the aforementioned pigheaded determination). Cumulatively, this knowledge has shaped who I am in a way that can only be described as life changing.

Success to me is the freedom to keep traveling, experiencing, and learning. It is also the right to ask dumb questions, to ask for things I am not entitled to, and to fall flat on my face—all in my quest to get to the next level of culinary enlightenment. And it wouldn't qualify as enlightenment if it didn't teach me to be less self-centered. I've been able to sweeten my life with the satisfaction of helping others, whether it means auctioning off a dinner at my house for a few generous folks, or jumping on a plane and cooking for causes I feel passionate about.

In today's world of *Top Chef*, memories are short-term and success is fleeting. While I do my best to focus on what's ahead of me, I try to enjoy every minute of life's rich pageant, knowing full well that it could all disappear faster than I can burn a batch of croutons. And as the pendulum swings back and forth from success to failure, from bitter to sweet, and from punishment to decadence—having the opportunity to ride the current wave of culinary consciousness has been the ultimate reward for this adrenaline junkie who is also an unabashed Glutton for Pleasure.

The Way I See It #19

in the abstract art of cooking, ingredients trump appliances, passion supersedes expertise, creativity triumphs over technique, spontaneity inspires invention, and wine makes even the worst culinary disaster taste delicious.

-- **bob blumer**
Creator/host of The Surreal Gourmet on Food Network Canada. His other car is a Toastermobile.

This is the author's opinion, not necessarily that of Starbucks. To read more or respond, go to www.starbucks.com/wayiseeit

thank-yous

IN MY QUEST TO ASSEMBLE AND UPDATE MY FAVORITE RECIPES AND ADVENTURES FOR THIS BOOK, I AM ESPECIALLY INDEBTED TO—

Kate Zankowicz, my effervescent amour, fellow gastronaut, and editorial fairy.

Suzi Varin, whose unique eye for all things edible turns every photograph into a study of form, color, and texture.

Elizabeth Karmel, my kindred culinary spirit and coauthor of *Pizza on the Grill*, with whom I have collaborated on many recipes, and from whom I have absconded with many, several of which appear in this book.

For the food photography sessions: Kristina Shires—digitizing, Kara Mickelson—kitchen assistance, Michelle Smith—P.A.

All my friends at Whitecap Books, the home of happy authors.

THIS BOOK WOULD NEVER HAVE SEEN THE LIGHT OF DAY WITHOUT THE GENEROSITY AND PATIENCE OF A LARGE CAST OF TALENTED CHEFS, PASSIONATE WINEMAKERS, ELOQUENT WORDSMITHS, BEMUSED FRIENDS, UNSUSPECTING NEIGHBORS, AND THE OCCASIONAL OUTLAW, WHOSE TUTELAGE FORMED THE BACKBONE OF MY 17-YEAR TRANSFORMATION FROM NEOPHYTE HOME COOK TO SELF-STYLED SURREAL GOURMET. I AM INDEBTED TO THOSE LISTED BELOW AND I APOLOGIZE FOR ANY NAMES THAT HAVE BEEN LOST IN THE CONTRAILS:

Alison Emilio, who led me to the door of the magic kingdom with the farfetched suggestion that I should write a cookbook.

Nion McEvoy, who allowed me to walk through that door instead of slamming it in my face.

Dick Kaiser, whose photos and creative collaborations from my first three books echo throughout this book.

My kitchen cabinet of chefs and foodies: David Sanfield, Mary Sue Milliken, Fred Eric, Marta Pan, Mary Burnham, Matt Zimbel, Gina Stepaniuk, Marc Collis, and Chris Macdonald.

Hall of fame testers: Waldo and Cherry Pesto, Judi Krant, Jow, Heidi "queen of the unmonied elite" Von Palleske, Audrey & Lily, and the babes: Julia, Kimberly, and Bridgette.

Wordsmiths: Aynsley Vogel (whose ongoing contributions to my professional life qualify her for sainthood), Colleen Woodcock, Mary Burnham, David Newsom, and Christopher Bird.

Graphic gods: Rodney Bowes, Kevin Reagan, and Sherri Hay.

SPECIAL THANKS:

Norman Perry for 15 great years of unwavering support and loyalty. Romily Perry, for seconding the motions. And Monica Netupsky for locking it down.

John Boswell, who during the time that he was my literary agent, wrote a cookbook called *A Man and His Pan*. I nicked his title for a section in this book.

Mary Beth McAdaragh and Ted Eccles (aka the man in the big yellow hat), for having the vision to turn the original Toastermobile tour into a TV show and launching *Surreal Gourmet*, Season One.

Dale Burshtein, for producing Seasons Two to Five of *Surreal Gourmet—and* upping the ante.

David Paperny, Cal Shumiatcher, Vera Lubimova, and everyone at Paperny Films, for being such excellent producers and creative partners in crime on *Glutton for Punishment*.

William Morrison, my director and off-camera coconspirator on *Glutton for Punishment*, for untangling me and my empty air tank from a bed of sea kelp 20 feet below the surface of Victoria Sound. And to all the others who have saved my life in the figurative sense.

All my friends at Food Network Canada and Discovery Travel & Living (Asia) and all the other networks around the world for carrying *Surreal Gourmet* and *Glutton for Punishment*.

Jane Siberry, Susan Rose, Barbara-jo McIntosh, Karen Gelbart, Suzanne Janke, Mary Ann Gilderbloom, and Sarah, Blair, Olivia, and Charlotte Damson.

Joan and "Gaucho" Jack Blumer—still with me in spirit.

And to the farmers, winemakers, and culinary artisans who make life delicious for those of us lucky enough to *live to eat*.

photography credits

suzi q. varin all food photography, kitchen still lifes, and portraits except as noted

george whiteside photo of Toastermobile on front flap

vera lubimova photo of Bob on back cover (taken moments after finishing third out of 200 teams at the Sonoma County Harvest Fair grape-stomping competition in Santa Rosa, California), as well as photos on pages 179 and 180

dick kaiser pages 33, 38, 46, 84, 124, 164, 166, 191, 193, 216, 224, 242, 249, 256, 266

bob blumer pages 231, 233, 234, 237, 238, 240, 272

index

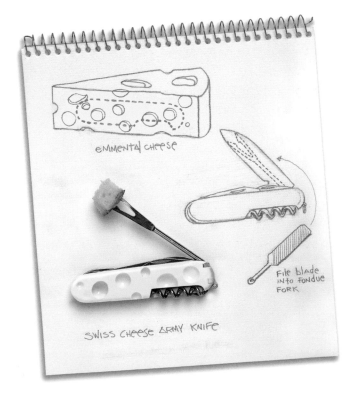

eMMeNTal cheese

File blade
iNto FoNDue
FoRK

SWiSS cheese ARMY KNiFe